# REIGNITE THE FLAMES

## FINDING OUR PASSION AND PURPOSE FOR LEARNING AMONG THE EMBERS

MANDY FROEHLICH

EduMatch Publishing

Published by EduMatch®
PO Box 150324, Alexandria, VA 22315
www.edumatchpublishing.com



These books are available at special discounts when purchased in quantities of 10 or more for use as premiums, promotions fundraising, and educational use. For inquiries and details, contact the publisher: sarah@edumatch.org.

# CONTENTS

# ENDORSEMENTS FOR REIGNITE THE FLAMES

*In her deeply empathetic book, Mandy Froehlich has curated some of the essential attributes for engaging educators at every level. On nearly every page are compelling stories, practical advice, and endless inspiration for reengaging with the love of learning and teaching.*

**— DANIEL H. PINK, #1 NEW YORK TIMES BESTSELLING AUTHOR OF *WHEN* AND *DRIVE***

*Powerful. Humbling. Insightful.*

*Sometimes our "why" and our purpose gets clouded by the environment we live in. Reading this book was exactly what I needed. As someone who got into education for all the right reasons, I have found myself, at times, feeling disengaged and frustrated. Mandy has helped reignite my flame by making me recognize my power to overcome both my perspective and my situation. If you have ever doubted your ability to make an impact or to keep going, this book could be what you are looking for to reignite the flame that is still lit somewhere within you.*

**— DAVE SCHMITTOU, EXECUTIVE DIRECTOR OF CURRICULUM AND INSTRUCTION, AUTHOR OF *BOLD HUMILITY* AND *IT'S LIKE RIDING A BIKE***

*I love this book! It is relevant, relatable, and important. Mandy does an incredible job of weaving together personal stories and the neuroscience behind why we feel certain things. She then provides us all what we need: permission to forgive ourselves for burning out or being beat down, and shows us how we can come back from it. There is so much real-ness and relevancy here, layered on a level of legitimacy. Whether you're fully engaged, or feeling burnt out, this book will impact you. Read it cover to cover, and then keep it close by. When you get beat down, let Mandy bring you back.*

— **JEFF GARGAS, COO/CO-FOUNDER, TEACH BETTER TEAM, CO-AUTHOR OF *TEACH BETTER***

*In this work, Mandy Froehlich has curated some of the most essential attributes for engaging learners at every level and shares them with deep empathy and tremendous impact in this work. Embedded within her book are countless vignettes, readily applicable actions for educators and students, and endless inspiration for reengaging with the love of learning and teaching.*

— **LINDSAY PORTNOY, PH.D., COGNITIVE SCIENTIST, ASSOCIATE TEACHING PROFESSOR AT NORTHEASTERN UNIVERSITY, AUTHOR OF *DESIGNED TO LEARN***

*This book came into my life when I thought it was time to leave the classroom. I was confused, lost, and heartbroken. I'd never imagined myself doing anything else. After reading "Reignite the Flames," I now have tools to center myself in what I once found passion in. It will take work, but I have the understanding and tools it will take to get my feet back on solid ground and make an informed decision on what's next.*

— **TEEA ROBINSON, 8TH GRADE ELA TEACHER**

*I do not consider myself a disengaged teacher, so when I began to read, Reignite the Flames, I didn't think it would resonate as much as it did. I realized there were moments in my career when I experienced disengagement and found that the strategies offered here are ones which I had used unknowingly and which I can now name and implement if this ever occurs again. More importantly, this book gave me a lens of empathy with which to support some of my peers who I now understand to be disengaged. Filled with research, personal anecdotes, and personal stories, this book is a must-read regardless of your educational context.*

— **JENNIFER CASA-TODD, TEACHER-LIBRARIAN AND AUTHOR OF *SOCIAL LEADIA***

# DEDICATION

*Thank you to the people who are required to love me, but I think they would love me anyway: Dan, Brycen, Goose, Cortlynne, and Addisyn. Thank you to Jackie and Jim for supporting me through college and making everything I've done possible since then.*

*Thank you to the people who aren't required to love me but still do it anyway: all of #My53s, Sarah Thomas, my friends and pseudo-family who have supported me through every weird idea I have. I didn't actually think I would ever be so lucky as to have people love me so much that never had to.*

*And finally, thank you to George Couros, whose keynote, book Innovator's Mindset, and friendship were the catalyst for my own re-engagement.*

# FOREWORD

*Jim Spoerleder*
*National School Trauma Responsive Trainer*

As educators and mental health professionals, we are living in a time where we are under overwhelming stress from demanding mandates coming from our federal, state, and school district levels. For too many, this overwhelming stress has robbed them of their passion and purpose that attracted them into their chosen profession. Mandy Froehlich walks us through the steps and process in which we can reignite the flames that brought us internal joy and satisfaction. As you read this book, you will discover that we can reclaim our passion and purpose through the embers and challenges that have caused us to question our career choice.

Mandy walks us through a process that helps us to see that with fire comes valuable lessons that make us stronger. Just as steel is put through the fire, it comes out on the other side with incredible strength and durability. As Mandy shares in this wonderful book of hope, we don't have to become victims of the fire; the embers do not have the power to cause disengagement unless we allow ourselves to become victims. Through this book, you will find that the embers can be a gift, a journey that creates an opportunity to strengthen us, and a pathway to walk through the flames and come out stronger than what we ever thought was possible. When we are able to maintain our focus, we are able to be present in the moment. We stay engaged and refuse to allow the embers to cause disengagement and rob us of the joy from living out our passion and calling. As Mandy connects with the reader, she provides the roadmap that keeps us focused on what's important and to adopt healthy self-care and social-emotional practices that offer support to stay the course.

I appreciate the practical approach that Mandy provides the reader, yet backed up with the science that should be driving our decisions. I believe as you read this book, your flame will shine

brighter, and your passion will continue to lead your journey to help bring hope and healing to those under your care. It is with gratitude that I support this book and the critical steps it offers us a path to wellness and engagement. My hope is that you will see the embers as valuable gifts to learn from and that they strengthen your engagement and commitment. If you have lost sight of your purpose, my hope is that you will see how the embers can cause disengagement if we fall into the fire and lose our sense of purpose and passion. My belief is that after you have read Reignite the Flames, you will be back on your path with a renewed sense of purpose and passion.

*Jim Sporleder retired in 2014 as Principal of Lincoln High School in Walla Walla, WA. Under Jim's leadership, Lincoln High School became a "Trauma-Informed" school, gaining national attention due to a dramatic drop in out of school suspensions, increased graduation rates, and the number of students going on to post-secondary education. These dramatic changes at Lincoln were recorded in the filming of the documentary, Paper Tigers, which tells the Lincoln story. Jim is currently working as a trauma-informed coach/consultant, keynote speaker, presenter, and trainer, and is based in Walla Walla, WA. Find out more about Jim at jimsporlederconsulting.com.*

# PREFACE

I can still remember the smell of my first classroom when I walked into it. The odor could be described as somewhere amidst the orange solvent they used for cleaning, the wax on the hallway floors that was wafting in, and the musty old building. It was my favorite combination. I didn't love every day of my job, and I didn't love every task I was assigned, but I did love teaching. I loved teaching so much that I did everything everyone asked of me. When I was able to take on more and do it well, I was asked to do more, and I did it because I knew it was good for the students even though I was tired and crabby with my own family when I got home. When people said, you're going to get burnt out, I said, "That's impossible. You can't get burnt out doing something you love." But you can. Too much of anything is still too much.

The person who said, "The hardest part is getting started," never woke up one day and decided that the profession that they had considered to be their life's calling was the same thing that was bleeding them emotionally dry. That moment for me was infinitely more difficult than getting started. When I began teaching, I had energy and endorphins and youth. When I disengaged and burnt out, I had growing kids of my own, not enough caffeine, and achy bones. I swear you age at two-times the rate as a teacher. And I was so unhappy.

If you asked me what success is, I would say it is being happy...whatever happiness means to that person. Continuing to grow and be better, yet still being content with how far you've come. I'd describe success as knowing you've made a positive difference in someone else's life. You understand what you bring to the table while still remaining humble. Success is looking back on your life, wishing you could do it all again the exact same way. And yet, being disengaged from your work or life isn't a way to do that. Engagement is a choice. Re-engagement is work. But I don't see any other way to be happy and feel successful within my scope of what happiness is. I don't see how losing your purpose can leave you with a life you'd do all over again.

The journey of discovering my own disengagement and researching the causes has given me a much more empathetic lens towards my fellow educators who are having the same feelings and experiences, possibly without even knowing it. It has made me more patient with those who have disengaged and made a target of their negativity. It has made me more aware of those who are starting to lose the light in their eyes and who have lost the magic—those who are tired and want out. It has made me reflect upon myself, my words, and my actions to understand how my own thinking impacts myself and those around me. It has made me want to support others because I feel like, at the end of the day, we all deserve and have the right to feel one of the most basic human emotions: happiness.

# I

# DISENGAGEMENT

When we separate ourselves from the things we love, we are also cutting out the passion and purpose in which we live our lives.

That, in itself, is reason enough to focus on re-engagement.

— MANDY FROEHLICH

# 1

# THE AWARENESS

Walk down the halls and look at your fellow staff. Really see your colleagues. Look at their faces, the slump in their shoulders, their half-smile in greeting, their eyes...can you even see them? Or are they downcast? Look at them when they don't think anyone is watching. What do you see? What is that perpetually grumpy fourth-grade teacher doing? The Calculus teacher who has had to be spoken to multiple times for the way they treat students? The instructional coach who spends professional learning time scrolling their personal social media accounts and complaining about the district? The principal with their head in their hands anxiously waiting for the next fire to start? Look at them in their quiet moments. Study them. Most likely, what you will see is the look of educator disengagement.

If we change the lens in which we are looking at these people, these humans, and recognize that people everywhere are fighting battles we know nothing about, we may be able to drum up empathetic feelings for these educators. I'm not saying this is easy. If the disengaged educators are your colleagues, they can be the same people who you've had negative interactions with yourself, who have even gone as far as to professionally bully you, who you've had to reprimand or have had your own day impacted by their behavior. Inevitably, in my mental health sessions and workshops when I ask for the participants to tell me the characteristics they think of when I say disengaged educator, no matter what part of the country I'm in, they describe these people the same way: leave the building right after school, complain about students constantly, argue against any type of change, ready to retire, and/or appear incredibly unhappy.

If these people sound like you, I'm so sorry for the state you're in. I hear you, sisters and brothers. While I will follow up this chapter discussing all of the ways our disengagement affects external factors, the reason I longed for re-engagement was from a very basic human need: to feel happy again. That was it. Did I want to help students and be the best teacher I could be? That was a part of it. Did I want to create change and have the energy to be relentless and tenacious when I believed change was needed? Yes, that was also true. But mostly, I was so tired of being angry and sad all the time. I believe that we all have the right to be happy in our jobs. We won't love every single task we have, and we will always be put into circumstances we don't like, but overall, I just wanted to love my job like I did when I first started. That's why I speak on educator disengagement—because we all have the right to love our jobs and be happy. To feel like we make a real difference. I feel that when educators are happy and engaged, the rest will fix itself.

I want to be clear that when I reference "educators" or "teachers" that I include administration in this group. Typically, I find that with administrators, one of their additional symptoms of becoming disengaged is forgetting their teacher's heart. Teaching is hard. So is administration, and they also can become disengaged if not careful...as can paraprofessionals, aides, secretaries, custodians, and student teachers.

## DEFINING DISENGAGEMENT

For a long time, we used the term disengagement to reference how well educators were paying attention to professional learning situations. My definition of teacher disengagement from *Divergent EDU: Challenging assumptions and limitations to create a culture of innovation* (Froehlich, 2018) is, "Educator disengagement is stronger than just not being interested in what you're learning or teaching at the time. It's the complete disconnection to the *why* behind teaching" I always considered this disconnection to be more like a form of selective amnesia—forgetting why you started in order to protect yourself from the reason(s) behind the disconnection. However, in diving deeper into educator disengagement over the last few years, I have expanded my definition. In psychology, **emotional disengagement**:

> "is a pattern of response, typically to negative emotional experience, that attempts to deny, suppress, or mask those resulting negative feelings. It can be manifested in a number of behaviors, but the goal is to remove oneself from the unpleasantness of those emotions, regardless of the consequences."
>
> — (ELLISON, 2017)

If you've ever experienced disengagement, this may sound familiar. You may have pulled back from teaching because the emotional toll it takes has forced you to cut emotional ties. You may have become so demoralized that it's easier to not care than it is to be hurt over and over. You may be dealing with issues outside of education that require what little energy you have left to be funneled there: divorce on the horizon, a sick child or parent, your own mental health issues. While there can be strategies to help with emotional disengagement, the initial reactions can be unintentional, much like I consider educator disengagement to be. When I mention the incredible impact that disengagement can have on the climate and culture, educators go immediately on the defensive and begin to passionately explain how they can't be responsible for everything, but I don't believe disengagement to be the "fault" of anyone. It's the possible result of working in a profession that is emotionally taxing and hard. When we say, "we have the ability to impact a child's life," it can have a positive or negative connotation depending on the day. I don't believe disengagement is intentional. It's not anyone's fault.

Therefore, in considering the definition of emotional disengagement and coupling it with what I know about the education profession, this is the definition I have developed:

***Educator disengagement*** *is the unintentional detaching of oneself from the emotional connection to the why behind education and teaching due to negative factors and/or circumstances that feel out of one's control. This results in an otherwise uncharacteristically negative view of their efficacy, jobs, and potentially their personal selves.*

The importance of defining educator disengagement is in helping others understand that the act of becoming disengaged is not a conscious choice. Nobody needs to feel like it's their fault.

However, re-engagement is possible, and just because something isn't your fault, it doesn't mean that getting better isn't your responsibility.

## DEFINING ENGAGEMENT

Forbes defines employee engagement not as happiness or satisfaction, although those may be felt in engagement, but as "the emotional commitment the employee has to the organization and its goals" (Kruse, 2012). Because education isn't a corporation, even though we can take some of its definitions and strategies as guides or lessons, retrofitting this idea into educator engagement means that we need to adjust the definition. What this does tell us is that even in the seemingly sterile atmosphere of the business world (as opposed to the more emotion-tied public servant jobs), emotion and engagement are still linked.

The term emotional engagement is often used in marketing. Marketing research has shown that when advertising is aimed at emotional engagement (making customers feel) versus logical engagement (showing them the data), they are four times more likely to purchase a product (Magids, Zorfas, & Leemon, 2019). Emotions are what drive human behavior. In terms of education, we can claim that great educators understand best practices in using data and teaching strategies and behavior strategies (logical engagement), and this may also be true, but I would challenge that emotion drives nearly everything we do (emotional engagement) and has the largest impact on our practices and the connections we forge with the students and our colleagues.

For example, as educators, we may be able to relate to this

situation: we have used the most effective strategies we know to work with a student who has been working diligently on improving their math scores, which have been an ongoing issue. They don't know their multiplication facts and look desperately around at their peers, embarrassed as they try to work through their tables. We have employed intense math interventions and parental support and spent recesses and lunches working extra to help boost the student's abilities. When we receive their test scores, their data, what it shows will elicit an emotional response. If the child is successful, we are excited and feel a greater sense of efficacy, the student's eyes light up, and they develop a greater appreciation for their hard work and more confidence in their math tables, and the parents are joyful at all the hard work that has gone into the improvement which has resulted in a happier child at home. If the child is unsuccessful, it may elicit feelings of never-ending struggle, that nothing makes a difference, and of failure. All of these are an emotional response, and while best practices will tell you the next appropriate step to take, they cannot provide you with the heart in which you engage with it.

Need more adult-centered examples? Think about how the emotion of finding out your child was severely sick, but you couldn't leave work because of the sub shortage, and how that affected the rest of your day. Or how much happier you were when a parent randomly brought you a cup of coffee in the morning and how that impacted your interactions with other parents you needed to contact. Think about the emotional response you have when a student from your "best class ever" reaches out 10 years later and invites you to their baby's baptism, and how that memory drives your interactions with your current students that day. Our emotional engagement impacts the decisions we make and our engagement in our work, regardless of the data and information that has come to us in a day. Even when we do learn a new teaching strategy, we are only excited about it if we really believe it will help a child learn (emotional). The fact that it might raise test scores is always secondary.

Emotional engagement can be positive or negative. Being frustrated, disappointed, or irritated is still being emotionally engaged. For both employee engagement and educator engagement, the positive emotions are obviously the ones that will drive connection and commitment. Because educators get into the profession to make a difference, the definition of educator engagement needs to include a more overarching, intrinsic goal of finding and living within your purpose. Therefore, the definition of educator disengagement that I propose is:

***Educator engagement*** *is intentionally seeking purpose and understanding our impact, living within that purpose, and creating opportunities for both ourselves and others to be happier, healthier, and more positively, emotionally engaged people in order to best serve those around us.*

While educator disengagement can happen unintentionally, staying engaged in education is a purposeful act. It involves empowering ourselves to understand how our emotions drive our decisions, finding and living within our purpose, developing our core beliefs that align with our purpose, and being self-aware. Figuring it all out takes a great deal of intention, and part of re-engaging is understanding that personal empowerment is intrinsically motivated. It can be a difficult undertaking to be engaged, especially if you're already wrestling with disengagement, but like with anything hard, the results are worth it.

## THE CONTINUUM OF ENGAGEMENT

Engagement and disengagement are on a continuum. One is not either completely disengaged or engaged, and the level of engagement can waiver depending on external factors (family matters, health) and normal progressions of a school year (testing time, breaks). For example, an educator's engagement in September when just coming back may look different than in *Farch* (a combination of February and March), which even the sound of the word correlates to exactly how it can feel. Engagement is more like an average; how you feel over the course of the good times and the bad. It's understanding that some periods will be difficult, but overall, you still are living within your purpose and understand your impact, and that drives you through the hard moments. The process of disengaging and subsequent re-engaging reminds me of the process by which people grieve. Even though grief is a process and certain stages can be predicted, the actual course it takes can be different for everybody.

As previously mentioned, emotional engagement can be described with positive and negative emotions. When looking at the educator engagement continuum, the opposite of engagement isn't anger and disappointment or sadness. If you're angry about something, you are still emotionally engaged. You still care about what happens, you're just feeling so many negative emotions that it feels like change is impossible even when it seems to be in the best interest of the students. I think there is a common assumption that you are either happy or not happy in your job. And if a continuum were created, many people may place happy and sad or angry at the opposite ends of the spectrum. Even if you'd go as far as to say you love your job, some may place hate at the opposite end. But I don't believe either of these to be true. I think that the opposite of happiness or love is instead apathy.

Disengagement is a complete disconnection. When you are sad or angry, it means that you are still passionate, and you care. I believe this to be true about many things, not just the engagement you feel in teaching. I feel like it's true about life in general. When you feel numb towards something and the care is gone, you have truly, completely lost your why. *There's no reason to be mad about the situation because nothing matters anyway. Colleagues will do what they do, and it doesn't impact practice, and students will continue not to care and will earn the grade they get.* That is complete disengagement. Emotional engagement tells me I'd most love to be happy, but my second choice would be to be angry because I would know that I still feel passionate enough to fight for what I believe. Apathy on the other hand...I've felt that. It's a hopeless, lost feeling. And if you feel like nothing you do matters, where would you even get the energy to try?

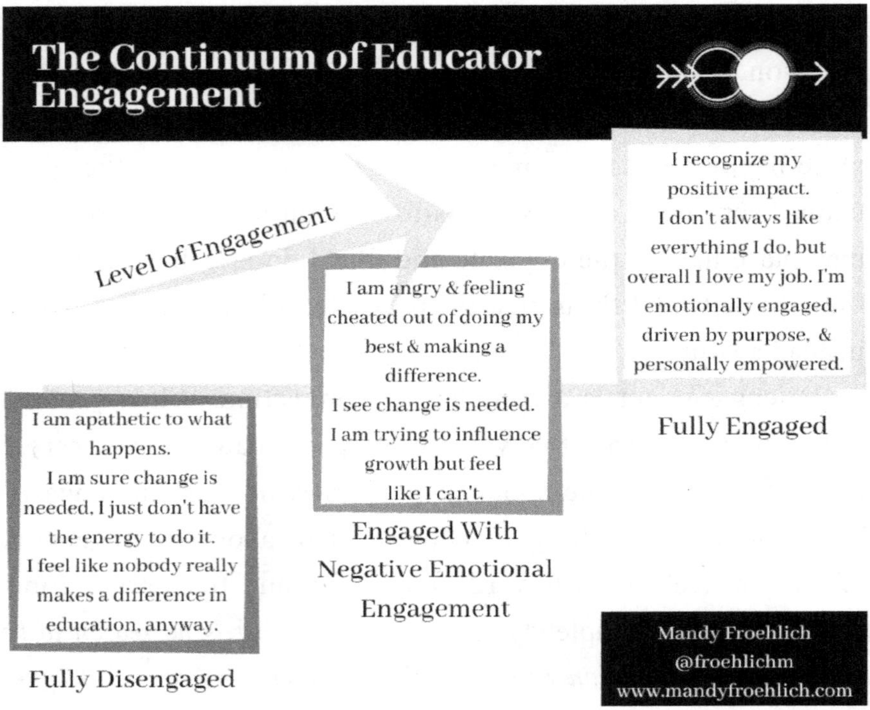


Figure A: The Continuum of Educator Engagement. Froehlich (2019).

## THE IMPACT OF DISENGAGEMENT ON CLIMATE AND CULTURE

The climate and the culture of a building has a high correlation to the engagement of the staff if you drill down to the core of issues and the catalyst for those problems. If the staff is high on the engagement continuum, the culture will be more robust, and the climate will be more positive. Engaged, purpose-filled people understand the need for connection and the importance of efficacy. If the climate and culture are weak and negative, there will be more educators that would fall closer to the disengagement side of the continuum. It only makes sense. If I'm feeling apathetic to what I'm doing, I don't care about creating relationships or being involved with others—it is going to negatively affect the climate and culture.

The one caveat is that it's a chicken or egg situation—does a negative climate and culture breed disengagement (I'd argue yes), or does disengagement determine the climate and culture (I'd still argue yes)? I believe that because climate and culture can be influenced by many factors, depending on the situation, both can be true. However, I believe one of the greatest influences on climate and culture is engagement.

When I developed the Hierarchy of Needs for Innovation and Divergent Thinking for *Divergent EDU* (2018), educator engagement was placed as one of the markers for climate and culture because a strong foundation of climate and culture has engaged educators. With holes in that foundational level, all the levels supported will not be as strong. Disengaged educators, for example, are less likely to take on positive leadership roles. They are less likely to be interested in mindset shifts, professional learning opportunities, or any kind of divergent and innovative thinking. It is impossible to be both a divergent educator and be entirely disengaged. Thinking and teaching divergently take passion and interest in education, which a lack of these connections is a hallmark of disengagement.

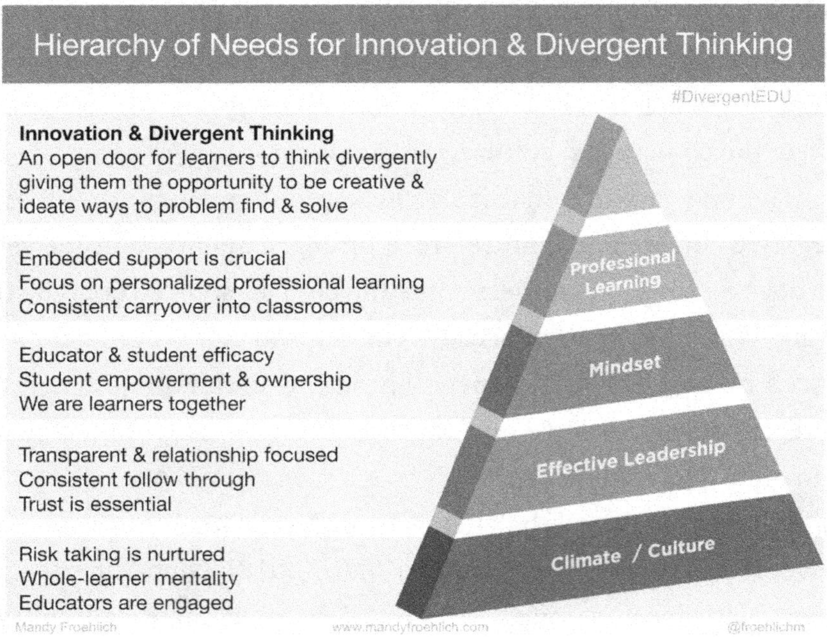


Figure B: Divergent EDU (2018)

## LOOKING AHEAD

*Reignite the Flames* is the follow-up book to *The Fire Within: Lessons from Defeat that Have Ignited a Passion for Learning*, in which I just begin to address educator mental health and disengagement. Part One defines emotions, engagement, and negative feelings that in the past felt foreign and unrecognizable, like disengagement. I introduce The Continuum of Educator Disengagement, and discuss the correlation between disengagement and climate and culture and how that relates back to the Hierarchy of Needs for Innovation and Divergent Thinking. Chapter Two builds on the categories of reasons why educators disengage in order to name them and, subsequently, learn to move forward.

Chapter Three dives into how the brain functions and reacts to stress and what happens inside our bodies if we do not heal ourselves emotionally and mentally.

Once we know how to define disengagement and how our body reacts to stress, Chapter Four digs into finding purpose and core beliefs and how they relate to re-engagement. Strategies for re-engagement are introduced in Chapter Five, and Chapter Six brings back discussion of the brain and body but in the context of positivity and gratitude. In the final chapter in Part II, Chapter Seven addresses mindfulness as a powerful tool to help calm the mind and destress, and how whole-person self-care is a necessity for maintaining balance. Tools and strategies for practicing mindfulness and self-care are also included.

In Part III, Chapter Eight addresses steps that buildings and districts can take to support educators and begin the discussions that will destigmatize mental health issues in a meaningful way. Chapter Nine, to round out the book, features powerful stories from brave students who were willing to share their struggles so we, their mentors and teachers, can best serve them.

2

# REASONS FOR DISENGAGEMENT

There was a specific moment when I became acutely aware of the feeling that would become my new normal for an entire year. My heart was beating overtime and I was breathing heavily, unable to catch my breath while sitting perfectly still. Sweat started to drip down my neck, under my collar, and down my back. My stomach rumbled like it was retaliating against my lunch, and while I felt totally overwhelmed and exhausted, the adrenaline was at least keeping me from putting my head on my desk and going to sleep. *How did I get here? I used to love my job.* I couldn't shake the feeling, and it made it worse that I knew I couldn't leave the profession. I had bills to pay and a family that needed medical insurance. I was trapped. I leaned back in my desk chair and bumped my head on shelving behind my desk, which caused an enormous stack of ungraded papers to fall haphazardly to the floor, and I started to cry.

Many of us have heard of the high attrition rates of our chosen profession. In 2015, the Center for American Progress estimated teacher attrition after the first five years to be at about 30% in the U.S. (Hanna & Pennington, 2015). In other places, the statistics are similar: 30% in English state schools (Weale, 2016), 50% in Australia according to the Hunter Institute of Mental Health (Singhal, 2017), 30% in Canada (Karsenti & Collin, 2013), and 28% in U.S. accredited schools in South America (Desroches, 2013). The statistics show that approximately one in every three teachers leaves the profession in the first five years, and this is not only a U.S. issue. It's a systemic educational issue which partially stems from the expectation that people will continue to work in a field where their passion is enough to fuel them through, and their expectation for reward should be little more than "making a difference."

What we usually fail to recognize when we discuss high attrition rates is the number of educators who need to stay in the profession because they can't make the choice to leave. They have families, bills to pay, mortgages, and car payments so they can get to work. Even though they told me in college that I could get a job anywhere as long as I just had a degree, when I disengaged, I found that's not necessarily true. We have people who want to leave the profession who are still in classrooms, forced to stay for various, legitimate reasons.

In 2018, I released a poll on Twitter that asked, "Have you ever thought seriously about leaving the education profession?" While I understand that it's not hardcore data, I was shocked when 72% of 1,281 respondents replied yes. I consider educators on Twitter to be closer to the engaged educator than disengaged as they are still trying to learn, which means that out of 1,281 engaged educators, there were still nearly three out of four who considered leaving. Teaching is hard. There is a tremendous amount of pressure in a profession where you have the capacity to contribute to the making or breaking of another human's future. That being said, the number of people who were still in education to answer the question suggested that there is the hope of re-engagement.

The term disengagement is an umbrella term for an outcome

that is a result, reaction, or symptom of a variety of possible causes. There are probably a million different combinations of scenarios that might cause disengagement. Multiple different factors can combine to cause complete disengagement. There are some common reasons, however, that are helpful to understand so that in the case of one approaching disengagement, they can recognize what's happening before it sets in. Or, if you're already disengaged, naming where you are may help you find your way out.

## PERSONAL ADVERSITY AND TRAUMA

Adversity is a difficult situation that causes struggle. Trauma is defined as "the response to a deeply distressing or disturbing event that overwhelms an individual's ability to cope, causes feelings of helplessness, diminishes their sense of self and their ability to feel the full range of emotions and experiences" (Onderko, 2018). The difference between trauma and adversity really depends on the person who is going through the experience, how they internalize what has happened, and their ability to cope. For example, in the case of a divorce, the divorce could be a traumatic experience for one spouse and a difficult adversity for another.

In either case, personal adversity and trauma can cause disengagement as all of the attention and energy need to be moved to the situation that's happening outside of work. In personal adversity or trauma, the reason for disengagement might not have anything to do with work at all, but that doesn't mean that the emotional toll that the personal adversity or trauma takes doesn't impact work. While we can claim that we shouldn't bring our personal issues to school, the reality is that while we may be able to keep the most intense emotions controlled, staying passionate about teaching while dealing with personal adversity or trauma is unrealistic. There is simply not enough energy in the tank sometimes to fuel both personal adversity or trauma and professional passion and engagement.

> Personal issues that may cause disengagement due to adversity or trauma:
>
> Care of aging parents | Challenges with children
> Death of a loved one | Serious health diagnosis
> Pending Divorce | Financial difficulties
> Time constraints due to the necessity
> of working multiple jobs.

## PROFESSIONAL ADVERSITY

Professional adversity is an event or situation that happens at work that causes struggle. This could be in the form of an emotional struggle, difficult student mental health challenges, bullying, a negative climate or culture, or it could be physical challenges that cause an emotional detachment like working long hours that cause exhaustion. Many times, if professional adversity is the issue, there are usually several difficulties that happen simultaneously. Professional adversity can also be the catalyst for personal adversity if the emotions spill over at home, which is likely. It's difficult to keep them totally separate when we have such an emotional connection to education.

There are a few common adversities that happen in educational settings that I believe we have the power to alleviate so that nobody has to disengage because of these issues.

### *Toxic Climate and Culture*

What I find interesting about a toxic climate and culture is that in order for them to be present and continued, there need to be people in the situation who are (either subconsciously or consciously) perpetuating them. I can say with nearly complete certainty that even the people who continue the negative, disconnected atmosphere don't like the way it feels. They may be accustomed to it, but it doesn't feel good.

I once spoke with an elementary staff about their negative climate and culture. I would have placed 90% of the staff on the continuum at either *engaged with negative emotional engagement* or completely *disengaged*. When I said, "The climate and culture of this building can be better, but you need to be the ones to choose to make it that way. I can't imagine wanting to work in a building that feels so suffocating, but working this way is a choice. By collectively making the decision to develop changes that will make the climate and culture more positive and then personally empowering yourself to these changes and keep each other accountable, you can turn the tide."

*Crickets.*

While I believe what I said to be true, the staff was either in a space where they didn't care (disengaged apathy), or they blamed other people for what was happening and they were angry about it (negative emotional engagement). Their level of engagement was hampering their ability to look at their circumstances objectively and try to find a solution. Until we addressed their engagement, there was going to be very little change in the climate and culture, yet this same issue in climate and culture could be the reason that the engaged teachers might begin to struggle and move down their own path of disengagement. In this case, the questions are:

- How do we kindly and purposely bring this to the attention of the staff?
- How do we support staff members where they are, and help them become more engaged from wherever their starting place is?
- How do we make the climate and culture the responsibility of everyone, while still providing disengaged staff the support they need to re-engage?

### *Workplace Bullying*

Workplace bullying is a topic that we often don't want to discuss because, as adults, especially educators, we don't want to believe that other adults would treat people in a way that would be considered bullying. Especially when we are constantly asking our students not to behave this way.

When I experienced workplace bullying, it sent me back to any adolescent feelings of exclusion, embarrassment, and the inability to prove myself no matter what I did. All my insecurities would come flooding back the second I'd walk into the building, knowing that I didn't get there early enough to avoid the bully and I'd be forced to interact with them, inevitably ruining the rest of my day. What made matters worse was that some days she was polite and nearly kind to me, making me question my sanity and the way I was reading the situation. Other times, especially in staff meetings, I was made to feel like every idea or opinion I had was unpopular through both comments and nonverbal cues. I walked around in a fog of anxiety and insecurity, and it took a massive toll on my self-confidence as I became quieter and less involved with the staff. An entire year of feeling like this was one of the reasons I initially began to disengage.

Unfortunately, just like bullying between kids, the act of bullying is usually related more to the insecurities of the bully than it has anything to do with the victim. Because of this, it is just as difficult as an adult to deal with this type of behavior because, as a victim, we have little to no influence over someone else's issues. I've had friends who have been professionally bullied who have instituted every suggestion that we would typically give students, and *they haven't worked.* The bullying didn't stop. Frankly, the bullying protocols we typically have in place don't really protect the victim, and as an adult, we rarely have protection because adults should "be able to take care of it."

Adult bullying can be detrimental to climate and culture and wreak havoc on the victim's mental health. A toxic climate and culture don't always include workplace bullying, but where you find workplace bullying, you will typically find a toxic climate and culture. If there is a bully, there is usually more than one person being bullied, and even the bystanders feel uncomfortable. It can impact a large number of the staff.

### *Absence of Professional Learning Opportunities*

The absence of professional learning opportunities can affect engagement because, in general, educators are interested in learning. Having the opportunity to connect with others that are able to give them ideas and strategies to be better for their students is a benefit of the job. If engagement includes knowing your purpose, then professional learning is one way to support that. The love of learning is a hallmark of being an educator. Take their own learning away, and you're starving part of what feeds our purpose and passion.

Another way that this can contribute to educator disengagement is when a new initiative requires professional learning that isn't provided with fidelity or worse, at all. With new initiatives or district expectations, educators want to know why they're doing it and how to do it well. They don't want cheap, non-existent, or weak professional learning, so they are not able to effectively and consistently conform to the initiative and apply their learning to their jobs. The lack of professional learning opportunities can add to the feeling that it's one more thing they need to learn on their own in order to live up to their own high standards for their teaching. If we want teachers to create robust, engaging, and focused learning in their classrooms, we need to respect them enough to provide them with similar professional learning opportunities that do the same.

### *Failure to Provide Support for the Risk-Taking Cycle*

When an educator doesn't feel supported in the risk-taking cycle, or worse, is reprimanded for failure when the district is supposedly moving towards innovative and divergent thinking, the non-support or reprimand can be a cause of disengagement. This happens because there is a disconnect between what is said (we want innovative ideas) and what is done (don't do it wrong or we will reprimand you), which creates fear and uneasiness to try something new even though the message is that's exactly what should be done. Risk-taking is an entire cycle of actions that all need to be supported, especially if the outcome of the calculated risk is a failure. Support throughout the entire cycle, even during failure, can help an educator feel like their effort is appreciated, and the personal cost for trying something new is worth it.

LEADERSHIP SUPPORT FOR THE RISK-TAKING CYCLE

**Idea for risk is determined**

A light bulb moment occurs. The established culture is supportive of new ideas and leadership models innovative implementations that may or may not fail. The idea keeper decides to give the risk an assessment for possible success..

**Risk and potential failure are assessed**

Any risk should include an assessment of the chance for success and what choices will be more likely to be successful. An appropriate support in this stage would be collaboration with experts encouraged by leadership or time to research the possible outcomes for larger risks.

**Risk is taken**

Moral support in the form of recognition with an email, staff recognition for the innovative thinking, or attending the risk to be a cheerleader would be examples of support at this stage. Encouragement and a smile are always appropriate. Acknowledgement of trying something innovative and divergent is imperative.

**Failure happens**

If the risk is unsuccessful, the support offered in this stage will determine if the risk-taker learns and moves forward or quits. The risk-taker might be angry, sad, self-defeated, or practicing negative self-talk. They will need positive support and encouragement along with possible collaboration to determine what iteration should be tried next.

**New iteration is tried**

The risk-taker may be determined to succeed but sensitive to another failure. Support needs to continue in the form of guidance and possible colleague involvement. There should always be the message, "We've got your back."

DIVERGENT EDU

MANDY FROEHLICH WWW.MANDYFROEHLICH.COM

## *Teacher Trauma*

Many of us can agree that the state of education and the fears that grip teachers and administrators have shifted. While we are not accepting of violence, as a society, we have become desensitized to it. In the past, the thought of a shooter in schools would be unfathomable, and the idea of a student beating a teacher would be absurd. We don't live in that world anymore.

I still find it unbelievable that we don't just practice in case of accidental fire, we practice for another human being to enter a building with the intention of shooting children. It sounds incomprehensible that there should be a plan for that. I was in a district that had an active shooter drill that involved police to come into the school with airsoft guns to shoot at teachers as they tried to escape the building. They were asked to follow a few directions but, overall, use their professional discretion as to which way they would run or if they would choose to fight or hide. When I was walking through the library after the drill, I came across a teacher who, truth be told, I really didn't know very well. She looked at me, glassy-eyed, and nodded. I asked her if she was ok and she replied, "I turned right. I should have turned left, but I didn't. I turned right, and me and all my kids were shot," and then she started to cry.

I recently presented my Show Must Go On mental health session to a group of educators. I asked them to raise their hands if they had been shot at with fake ammunition by authorities during drills. Out of a room of approximately 100 people, roughly half of them raised their hands. This is not an isolated incident.

I can't imagine the damage we are causing by participating in drills where this is the outcome. I have heard the authorities say that we practice committing the actions to "muscle memory." While I believe conversations need to happen where we discuss what to do, and creating plans is responsible, shooting at anyone in the name of muscle memory is creating more damage than it is helpful. A person needs to practice something hundreds of times to commit it to muscle memory, and in the case where we are in different areas of a building at any given time, we would need to practice what we are going to do in any of those areas that many times. Regardless, the threat of being the person responsible for protecting 25 or more children that are not ours with our own life is significant. The practice and mindset needed to be ready to protect them can be emotional in itself, and without the appropriate coping skills, it can become a teacher trauma.

I am not an advocate for ignoring active shooter preparation. I believe that walking through plans, listening to announcements, practicing the activation of the alarm are all appropriate. I even think a solid case can be made for listening to gunshots in different parts of the building. This can be helpful as sometimes the way that sound travels can be misleading (although I still think this can be traumatic for some people). Ignoring the possibility of an active shooter is irresponsible, but I also think many of our current practices are not rooted in common sense and instead are creating more trauma than the preparation they're providing.

Another kind of teacher trauma has to do with students who have behavior that is verbally or physically violent or abusive. One of the first times this was brought to my attention was with a paraprofessional who was working with students with behavior challenges. She had just gotten back from the hospital because a student had bitten her until it bled, and she needed a tetanus shot. When I asked to see where she had been bit, she lifted up her sleeves and showed me, but what I noticed beyond the bite were the bruises that covered her arms and hands. I gasped, and she told me that the students that she works with "hit and kick her often."

I want to preface what I'm about to say with this: I fully understand that we have students who have a difficult, if not impossible, time controlling their behavior or their bodies. I do not say this to be insensitive to their challenges.

As a district, we need to provide more supports for people in these positions, so they are able to take breaks and tag team. When people are verbally or physically assaulted regularly, that is called abuse, even if it is a child to an adult. Nobody should be expected to go to a job, much less engaged in it, if they are continuously being abused in that setting without additional support in place to alleviate some of the stress from being put in such a position.

### *Uncontrollable Circumstances*

I have been fortunate in my career to never have a student in my direct charge pass away. I can't imagine the pain caused by spending so much time with a child who is one day there, and the next day gone. And because we are the caregivers, our own emotions are put aside to help everyone else. This can also be true of secondary relationships such as school counselors, administration, or specialists. The loss of a child in any school setting is traumatic. If we are told to love our students and to act *in loco parentis,* and many of us take that very seriously. Many times, the teachers and other educators are so busy trying to take care of their students and community in the face of a tragedy that they forget to process their own feelings, which can leave a hole that is never addressed.

## ON THE LOSS OF A CHILD

Rachel Seevers
School Counselor, Wisconsin

There wasn't a class that taught me how to prepare for losing a student or delivering the message of their death to the rest of the school. These two tasks have been the most difficult part of my career as a School Counselor in a rural Wisconsin High School. Last school year, I was notified by one of my students, one that I have a close family connection with, that her cancer had been labeled incurable. When she shared her prognosis, I was at a loss for words. I knew that I needed to find them, though, because I was going to have to tell my staff that we were going to be losing a beautiful 17-year-old soul to a horrible illness. As difficult as this was, I kept telling myself that I could handle it because she wasn't MY child. I found the courage and shared the news at our staff meeting. You could have heard a pin drop after I was done speaking.

Throughout the school year, I updated my staff as often as I could about the progression of her illness, knowing that someday soon, I was going to have to deliver the worst news of all. As that day was quickly approaching, I reached out to another high school counselor from a neighboring district and asked for her help. I shared the student's situation with her so that when the day came, someone could just call her, and she could support the students with me. Knowing that I was going to have someone else trained in mental health available to support my students alleviated a lot of my apprehension. I didn't have to feel solely responsible for providing support to my students...because *what if I couldn't?*

Sadly, that day came in the middle of May. We called an all-staff meeting during our school's breakfast break, and I shared the news that we had lost her. I also shared that we had mental health professionals here to support our students and staff should they need it. The staff had about 10 minutes together for this conversation and to deal with our own feelings before we had to head back to our classrooms.

Even though I knew that other adults in our building could help our students, I wanted her family and friends to be able to get support from me as well. I spent the remainder of that day giving out hugs and shedding tears with the students. I believe those tears were more out of empathy for their loss than my own grief because I had

shut a part of me off to support them. Because I suppressed my feelings all day, I was too exhausted to process them when I got home. I went to bed early to be ready to do it all over again the next day. It was a week after she passed that I realized that I didn't take the time to process my own grief, or any emotion for that matter. I had shut all of my sadness off in an effort to appear strong for my students. Educators are constantly doing whatever we can to support our students' academic and emotional needs, even at the cost of ignoring our own.

Teacher traumas can be the cause of disengagement as educators try to emotionally disconnect from the source of their trauma.

## DEMORALIZATION

I first learned about demoralization in the teaching profession through the book *Demoralized: Why Teachers Leave the Profession They Love and How They Can Stay* (Santoro, 2018). Santoro defines demoralization as a "more precise diagnosis of experienced teacher dissatisfaction...rooted in discouragement and despair borne out of ongoing value conflicts with pedagogical policies, reform mandates, and school practices." Education is different from most other professions as educators generally enter the profession with the feeling of a moral obligation to create positive change and make a difference.

Demoralization happens when policies, politics, initiatives, leadership, and the community create circumstances or an atmosphere where the educator feels like their moral obligation to make a difference is challenged. When they feel vilified for trying to do their best job with little community or political support, while paying for their own classroom supplies and making less money than they need to pay their bills, demoralization can occur. This is not the same as burnout. Symptoms of demoralization are (Watson & Kissaine, 2017):

- low morale
- reduced hope
- sense of feeling stuck, helpless, pointless or purposeless,

- doubts about the value of continued engagement in education.

Similar to re-engagement, Santoro (2018) states that remoralization can occur when the difference between burnout and demoralization is understood, and the difference in strategies to combat each is recognized and practiced accordingly.

## BURNOUT

Burnout has recently been recognized as a medically diagnosable syndrome by the World Health Organization and the medical community. In this case, it needs to be specifically applied to burnout in the workplace as opposed to burnout in one's personal life, but by recognizing burnout as a medical diagnosis, it allows people to get appropriate help when necessary (and have it covered by insurance if applicable). The symptoms of burnout are categorized by the World Health Organization (n.d.) as:

- feelings of energy depletion or exhaustion
- increased mental distance from one's job
- feelings of negativism or cynicism related to one's job
- reduced professional efficacy.

The similarities between several of the potential mental health issues can make it difficult to tell them apart. While the hallmark of demoralization focuses on low morale and reduced hope, burnout can also be described as emotional and physical exhaustion, accompanied by dread, impaired concentration that can get worse the longer it continues, a weakened immune system, in the early stages constant irritability and later, angry outbursts. Both burnout and demoralization can accompany other mental health issues like anxiety or depression.

## SECONDARY TRAUMATIC STRESS OR COMPASSION FATIGUE

I have a strange relationship with secondary traumatic stress or compassion fatigue. I learned about it while writing my first book, *The Fire Within,* and felt like it was an area we weren't recognizing in education, and yet it had to be an issue as our students were experiencing their own traumas and bringing them to school. I began researching, writing, and speaking on it at the same time that I became open publicly about my own Complex PTSD, depression, and anxiety. As the book was released and more people opened up to me about their mental health issues because I was modeling my own vulnerability, I developed secondary traumatic stress and was officially diagnosed a year later. This is proof that even having a deep knowledge about some of these issues does not preclude you from developing them if you don't remain careful and aware.

Secondary traumatic stress, also called compassion fatigue, vicarious trauma, or secondary trauma, is typically discussed in counselor or social worker circles as it is defined as "the emotional duress that results when an individual hears about the firsthand trauma experiences of another" (Peterson, 2018). Educators add another layer to the susceptibility to secondary traumatic stress as they care about their students, see them most days, and tend to be especially empathetic. In other words, because we worry about the students who go home and won't have dinner or the ones who have an abusive parent that Child Protective Services hasn't addressed, or the foster kids who have been bounced around from family to family, we have the ability to develop secondary traumatic stress. Note: developing secondary traumatic stress has nothing to do with our own experience with trauma. While the symptoms may manifest themselves differently if we have suffered trauma (particularly if we have Post-Traumatic Stress Disorder), the development of secondary traumatic stress is just as likely for someone who has not suffered trauma as it is for someone who has.

The symptoms of secondary traumatic stress mimic those of Post-Traumatic Stress Disorder (PTSD). Secondary traumatic stress does not give you PTSD—the symptoms just mimic it. Symptoms of PTSD (Administration of Children and Families) are:

**Cognitive**

- Lowered Concentration
- Apathy
- Rigid thinking
- Perfectionism
- Preoccupation with trauma

**Behavioral**

- Withdrawal
- Sleep disturbance
- Appetite change
- Hyper-vigilance
- Elevated startle response

**Emotional**

- Guilt
- Anger
- Numbness
- Sadness
- Helplessness

**Physical**

- Increased heart rate
- Difficulty breathing
- Muscle and joint pain
- Impaired immune system

One of the hallmarks of PTSD is disconnecting from the things you love the most. Therefore, if you love your job, chances are that it will be something you begin to disconnect from. Recommendations for warding against secondary traumatic stress include self-care and participating in activities that help to focus on maintaining identity to help remember who you are in times of stress.

***Social Media***

When our students become depressed or anxious over what is happening on social media, we warn them that everyone is always putting their best face forward, and images on social media are the best versions of someone on that day coupled with filters and editing. "You shouldn't compare your every day to their best day," we say. They are highlighting the good and filtering out the acne, and take 25 pics to get that one Instagram-worthy post. We tell our students not to worry about what is on social media and to just be themselves, and then we turn away from them to our computers and scroll social media and throw our own advice out the window by comparing ourselves to all the other social media-savvy educators.

Even after I became aware of engagement and found myself working to re-engage, it was still difficult for me to get through my social media feed. In one way, I valued social media for the deep connections I had forged with my professional learning network and would not deny social media just for that reason. However, scrolling through all the amazing post-after-post, highlighting activities that I couldn't keep up with, made me feel like I wasn't working hard enough. I would read through Twitter and feel like what I was doing paled in comparison to what everyone else was doing, but I felt like I was working to the point of exhaustion every day.

Post: Listen to my new podcast!
Internal dialogue: *Ugh. We haven't recorded a podcast lately.*
(concerned-face)

Post: Read my article that I wrote for this important online
education site!
Internal dialogue: *I wish I could write important articles.*

(sad-face)

Post: Look at this video my students made!
Internal dialogue: *Does what I do even really impact students?*
(doubting-my-efficacy-face)

Social media was becoming more and more of a burden to me instead of the place for growth that it had been a few years prior. However, my negative attitude flare-ups were happening because I was allowing it.

I've heard people talk about abandoning social media because they are tired of the filtered images, the celebrations, and bragging, but I am a firm believer that people should be able to celebrate their accomplishments, no matter how small they may seem to anyone else. That may be the biggest thing they've accomplished lately, and we all need to celebrate with them. If it makes us feel anything but pride and support, that is more about the way we are allowing social media to make us feel than it is about what the celebratory post is actually saying.

We have control over the way that social media makes us feel. Someone else celebrating an accomplishment shouldn't make us feel guilty or inept. If we feel that way, that's on us. When I started to understand that there are always stories behind every post and that I had control over the way that I allowed social media to make me feel, it was a game-changer in how I felt about myself in relation to the posts I was reading. It wasn't that everyone else was doing things that I needed to be doing more of, it was that the combination of all the posts that I read and saw were little goals that I may want to set for myself (or maybe not...

we can't do it all). We may not be able to control what others put on social media, but we can certainly change the way we think and feel about it, and being able to guide our emotions in healthier directions is one of the best ways we can move forward in the way we think and interact with both ourselves and with others.

This more positive view of people and posts helped with the stress that I was placing on myself to be better and do better. If we don't understand that we are responsible for how social media makes us feel, then we are more likely to disengage, as we feel like we can't compare to all the phenomenal educators on social media. While I don't believe social media to have the power to be the sole reason for complete disconnection, it can be a contributor when partnered with other issues.

> “We are not less because of what someone else has accomplished. Jealousy is more about insecurity than it is about success.
>
> — MANDY FROEHLICH

Knowing what we are experiencing and recognizing symptoms can at least help to know what we are dealing with. Also, understanding what can cause changes in levels of engagement with colleagues might help us look at them through a more empathetic lens and employ other strategies to create a more positive climate and culture that may help them elevate their engagement.

3

# THE BRAIN, BODY, AND EMOTION CONNECTION

The catalyst for the most recent return to counseling was an incident that happened with my eldest son. I was bringing him home from a physical therapy appointment for a college football-season-ending-before-it-started ACL injury, which had already crushed his spirit. I felt terrible for him, like any good mom would. But all that ended in the car on the way home when he triggered me with something he said regarding a long-discussed decision he had made, one which his dad and I disagreed with him. Vehemently.

It's important to note here that what he said was both unintentional and unimportant. It was irritating but not disrespectful, and still not that any of those things would have warranted my reaction. It may or may not have been something that would have triggered anyone else. But that didn't matter. It triggered me, and I was the one in the car.

I immediately entered a space where the rage I felt toward both him and the topic of our conversation was off the charts. I have learned in these rage cycles that seeing red is a real thing. I said things to my son, whose spirit had already been broken by his current circumstances, that I would never repeat intentionally to another human being. I was driving, yet blacked out and don't remember most of what I said or actually even driving home. The next thing I knew, we were in the house, and he was lying in bed crying, and I had enough adrenaline coursing through my veins to lift and throw several mid-sized vehicles. It was awful. And as I sat next to him and hugged him, apologized profusely, and listened to him cry, I vowed to never get to the point where I would do that again. I was scared but determined; mortified, yet resolved.

Fortunately for me, I have been dealing with mental health issues for so long that I am able to reason (after the fact) through what had happened. I knew these things:

1. I was able to name my emotion: rage. This helped me understand what I was dealing with.
2. I understood that even though I was embarrassed by my behavior, had a massive amount of remorse, guilt, and sadness, and wanted it fixed as soon as possible—as long as I worked toward healing and getting better, this did not define me or make me a bad person.
3. There was a trigger in that conversation that I needed to dive deeper into. I needed to determine why it was a trigger and what strategies I could use to work through similar triggers in the future.
4. I knew that I had activated the fight mode in my brain. It is a primitive response, and while activated, I could not rationalize what I was saying or doing.

Knowing all this does not mean that it's easier to emotionally digest in the aftermath. Knowing how the brain works is one of the first steps to understanding our emotions, reactions, trauma, and mental health. But, even though I understand how I felt when

I was there, it still feels like a cop-out to say, "I couldn't help it," even though it is true—I was not thinking with the rational part of my brain. However, and I'll say this again and again: just because it may not have been my fault, doesn't mean it's not my responsibility to apologize and heal.

Just because it may not have been my fault doesn't mean it's not my responsibility to heal.
MANDY FROEHLICH
#REIGNITETHEFLAMES
WWW.MANDYFROEHLICH.COM | @FROEHLICHM

Emotions can feel very abstract. For example, if I asked you what makes you truly happy, could you tell me? What if I asked about contentment or the difference between happiness and joy? Or the nuances between disappointment, anger, and rage? We refer to feelings of being in love or out of love, for example, as our heart exploding or being heartbroken. But we are well versed enough in our bodies to know that emotion doesn't actually come from our heart (even though in times of strong emotion, we can certainly feel it in our chests). We are often told to control our emotions, but unless we have been given strategies that work for us, we find it difficult (if not impossible). Subsequently, we may feel like we're failing at something we haven't been taught how to do because it feels like being able to control emotion should be an innate trait—something we just know how to do.

In reality, our emotions and reactions are one of our brain and nervous system's many functions. Our brain uses the connections it has made through our learning, experiences, perceptions, and relationships to determine how to feel and react. Our brains are pre-wired for survival, and no matter how much of an introvert one is, it is also wired to be social and function successfully in groups. When we act a certain way, it is a symptom of something that is happening in our brain and nervous system.

## A LITTLE LESSON IN THE BRAIN AND NERVOUS SYSTEM

To best understand how our emotional response is tied to our brain and nervous system, it's imperative to understand how they work. The brain's main concern, above all else, is survival. The brain registers our basic needs, helps us understand our environment so we can meet those needs, regulates our body so we can do what we need to meet those needs, and warns us and readies us for danger. Because we are human, which means we are mammals, our brain and nervous system are focused on how we can best survive and thrive in a group. All of those elements need to work together for us to function normally.

### *The Brain*

Our prefrontal cortex, located in the front, is the supercomputer for complex thinking. It begins to develop at the time we are born and continues until the age of 24. When we are activating our prefrontal brain, we are calm and in control. It allows us to listen to arguments and make decisions, and to be open and mature—it provides us with a sense of inhibition for inappropriate actions and allows us to be empathetic. It is what separates us from other animals.

The limbic brain, located right above the reptilian brain, is also known as the mammalian brain because all mammals have it. It is actually broken up into two pieces: the Neo-Limbic and the Paleo-Limbic brains. The Paleo-Limbic brain is deeply rooted and difficult to change. The actions in this brain are based on power struggles and our position in groups that are heavily influenced by self-confidence and trust. The result is whether we appear as dominant or submissive in any group situation. The Neo-limbic brain is the home to our deepest motivations and desires, and it's where memory and consciousness live. It houses all the complexities and paradoxes of personality and is shaped by both our genetic makeup and our experiences from the day we are born.

The most primitive part of our brain, sometimes called the reptilian brain, is at the base of our skull right in the brainstem. It's important to note that the brainstem is actually correlated with the entire nervous system below the neck (and includes the vagus nerve). It is our ancient animal brain and is responsible for everything that keeps us alive: breathing, eating, relieving ourselves, feeling temperature and pain. This primitive part of the brain cannot adapt or evolve. It does not have memories. This part of the brain and nervous system recognizes the difference between life and death, and switches to what the body needs in order for it to survive.

***Polyvagal Theory***

The Polyvagal Theory was introduced by Stephen Porges in 1994. Polyvagal refers to the many branches of the vagus nerve which connect numerous organs, including the brain, lungs, heart, stomach, and intestines. In *The Body Keeps Score,* the importance of the Polyvagal Theory is described as giving us, "a more sophisticated understanding of the biology of safety and danger, one based on the subtle interplay between the visceral experiences of our own bodies and the voices and faces of the people around us" (Van Der Kolk, 2014, p. 80). Basically, it explains why we react the way we do, what happens in our bodies, and how those reactions are intertwined with our social relationships.

In my first book, *The Fire Within* (2018), psychologist Dr. Elizabeth Rogers-Doll wrote how the Polyvagal Theory explains how our body process emotions and reacts to stimuli:

> Steven Porges has a complex theory about how human beings respond to the tiniest or greatest of life events. Our brains and bodies take in information through a process he calls neuroception. It is similar to the term perception. Neuroception is how "neural circuits (within us) distinguish whether situations or people are safe, dangerous or life-threatening" (Porges, 2013). My response to a terrible event may not be the same as yours. Nevertheless, each of our responses is validly our own. There are three different responses to threats that are guided by the vagus nerve. The vagus nerve is one of 12 cranial nerves that run throughout the body. Vagus is Latin for "The Wanderer," which describes how the vagus wanders all around the body (p. 196).

The vagus nerve is the mediator of our stress response. This theory explains how the autonomic nervous system regulates in three fundamental psychological states. The first level, social engagement, means we look for other people for help or assistance. We look for comfort or for someone else to help us regulate our emotions. If nobody is around or we are in immediate danger, we revert to flight or fight. If we are unable to run or fight off the danger, our body will shut down to preserve as much energy as possible. If that happens, we are in a state of freeze or collapse.

Neuroception "should" be calibrated "correctly" to differentiate between safety and threat. For example, if we grow up in a safe home where it's alright to feel embarrassment and disappointment, then these feelings will be activated and won't trigger a stress response. But if we don't grow up with this safety, these emotional triggers become correlated with a trauma response. This is faulty neuroception, and it makes us vulnerable to trauma triggers.

### *Survival Strategies*

The feeling of danger turns off our social engagement system, and our other survival strategies begin to take shape. According to Polyvagal Theory, the survival strategies that our mammalian brain uses are flight/flee and fight. The strategy of freeze and collapse are regulated by our reptilian brain. Most people have a preferred stress response. Stress reactions can change, and someone triggered can experience several of the reactions, even going through all of them within a few minutes. The perceived danger needs to be taken away in order to take away the need for a defensive reaction. This will put the reptilian brain back in standby mode.

**Flight/Flee.** During flight/flee, the brain accelerates the heart rate and sends blood to the legs in order to prepare to be able to run away quickly. Someone who is in this mode may have a repetitive movement such as tapping feet or shaking hands, and often have eyes that seem to be moving and can't focus because they're looking for an escape route.

A person in flight/flee should not be told to calm down. They will take it as a constraint, and since they are already trying to escape the situation, this will exacerbate the issue. Instead, use open questions that show they are free to choose. Giving them options or asking them to take a walk to get rid of nervous energy can be helpful.

**Fight.** A person in fight mode has the objective to intimidate. They will show defensive aggression and feel like they need to crush the threat at hand. Fighting is about power. The neck, arms, and jaw will be tight; they will have marked tension in their body; their eyes will be staring or squinting; and they may be standing straight to show how powerful they are. Overall, the person will have a feeling of superiority. They will make their voice loud in order to make themselves feel more important. To help a person in this state listen without interruption, offer solutions quickly, get to the point, and be factual. Say things like, "If I were you, I'd be angry, too." Do not yell or question what is being said, or laugh at them. They are already aroused, and this will only irritate them more.

In fight or flight, we still believe we have the ability to survive whatever we perceive as danger.

**Freeze or Collapse.** Freeze and collapse are a form of self-preservation. Collapse is when our nervous system believes we are in a life-threatening situation and is trying to make us as still as possible. In freeze mode, the person will try to make themselves look as small as possible, so the perceived threat will overlook them. The brain slows everything down, and they may appear lethargic. Their eyes may be downcast or looking at nothing, hanging head, with desperate sighs. They may be crying. Their objective is to find a loving and caring individual to help them. In this case, telling them to "buck up" or "rub dirt on it" or work through it or some other version of being tough is the opposite of what they actually need. To help somebody in freeze mode, get on their level. Put an arm around their shoulders and offer small steps to move forward.

Being an educator, I'm sure that you have conjured up situations with students who have exhibited these behaviors. In all of the information that I just gave, the most important part to understand is that when the fear response is triggered, and someone is operating out of their reptilian brain, they are not in control of what they say or do. Everything is running on an automatic response to perceived danger. We might describe them as *out of control.* They are unable to think clearly or rationally about their choices or the consequences of their actions. It's not that they don't want to or are being obstinate, it's that biologically they have little control over their actions.

Ponder that for a second. What is the first thing we usually say to someone who has been triggered? *"Think about what you're doing! Does this seem like an appropriate way to act?"* Or for ourselves if we have been put into that kind of a situation: *"I should know better than that. What is wrong with me?"*

We are capable of worrying about something that might never happen. This may be particularly evident if you're a parent, and in many ways, being an educator has many of the same worries for our students. The concern doesn't need to be life-threatening. In fact, the fear response can be activated by something like speaking in public, which may be scary to one person but not to another depending on our personalities and past experiences. It is just the perception of danger. For example, in the case of stage fright, the trigger might be the fear of being embarrassed or doing something socially unacceptable, which, in turn, may cause the survival strategy of freeze to be enacted.

The perception of danger can also stop us from doing things that seem completely reasonable and which should not cause fear in normal circumstances. It can be what stops us from applying for a new job we want because we are afraid we won't get it. It can be a cause of procrastination if we are feeling afraid or overwhelmed at the tasks we need to accomplish. If we need to make a call to an angry parent or have a difficult conversation with the principal, we may procrastinate at scheduling the call and wait until the very last minute, even if our fear seems completely unfounded and irrational. This part of the system is not equipped to determine what is good or not good for us. It is only there to register our fear, which means that sometimes we need to be ready to acknowledge the fear and move through it anyway in order to do the things that will help us grow.

### *Stress*

Stress is any stimulus that requires us to change. Stress isn't inherently bad or negative, but when it becomes traumatic stress or overwhelming stress, that is when we encounter problems. Sustained overwhelming stress over a period of time can have a negative effect on the brain and body. In the brain, sustained stress will decrease dendrites in the hippocampus, which are connected to memory. The brain can also experience dendritic retraction and synapse loss in the frontal cortex where our supercomputer is housed. These changes lead directly to attention loss and decision-making impairment. Stress increases frontal motor connections and decreases hippocampus ones. Our brain is rewiring itself to fight off danger and run away and make sure we don't get too traumatized by remembering every possible moment should we get injured. Our brain doesn't understand that we don't always need that in today's world. Stress is everywhere. These changes can undermine neuroplasticity and our ability for our brain to function properly.

The body similarly reacts to chronic stress. Your nervous system can be thrown into a survival strategy, which can increase your heartbeat (which raises your blood pressure) and prepare your body to run, hide, or fight. Because muscles can be taut from the preparation, injuries and joint pain are more likely from the tension.

Extra glucose production to provide a boost of energy can increase the chance for Type 2 Diabetes. "The rush of hormones, rapid breathing, and increased heart rate" can also aggravate existing ulcers and cause a surge in acid production in your stomach (Pietrangelo & Watson, 2018). The immune system, over time, begins to deteriorate, which not only leads to getting sick easier, but also lengthens the time to get better when we do get sick.

Our reproductive systems can be affected as well. Men may find that with chronic, sustained stress, their testosterone levels are affected, which can cause reproductive and desire issues, insomnia, and exhaustion. It can also cause emotional dysregulation, including an increased risk of depression, reduced memory and concentration, and decreased motivation and self-confidence (Gotter, 2019). Women can also experience a loss of desire, and their menstrual cycles may be affected, which can lead to reproductive issues. Chronic stress may exacerbate menopausal symptoms (Pietrangelo & Watson, 2018).

### *Neuroplasticity*

Neuroplasticity is the process of our brains changing and creating new connections. The size and function of a brain are highly sensitive to the environment, which includes social interactions—the social interactions being perhaps the most highly influential aspect of the environment that determines how the nervous system/brain will develop. New experiences and interactions cause the brain to grow. Robbing it of new experiences or interactions or doing the same routines day and in and day out will affect the brain adversely.

The brain itself carries no judgment or moral compass. Whatever is done the most will be wired into the brain. Whatever we do most, our brains will adapt. The more we do something, the more synapses and dendrites will grow. The denser the neuronal network, the better we are at the behavior. Therefore, if you grow up in an environment that is happy and safe, you will be more likely to trust others and recognize happiness. If you are constantly scared and denied love, you are more likely to be plagued with feelings of fear and abandonment because these are the connections that your brain made. If you spend a great deal of your time in stressful situations, your brain will be wired to anticipate being stressed. I would categorize any job in education as stressful, so if you're not doing something to wire your brain for self-care, you're setting your brain up to make deep connections to stress. The beauty of neuroplasticity is that it's what allows us to change and grow with hard work and dedication to being better. I'll address that further in an upcoming chapter.

### *Trauma and the Brain*

When we experience teacher trauma or personal trauma, it changes our brain. Trauma is a distressing or disturbing event or experience that is beyond our emotional tolerances and coping strategies. Traumatic experiences affect our bodies in a way that takes away our ability to choose logic. That's the hallmark of trauma: the original situation reduces our choice instead of having the wide array of actions to choose from that is everyone's birthright (the full spectrum of anger, responsibility, fear, sadness, joy, and the millions of nuances in between). When our body learns that fighting or fleeing (for example) is the only choice, then that pattern of firing will change the structure of the brain, making it more likely that we will automatically activate that limited choice in the future in a way that is beyond conscious control.

Trauma is different for everyone because everyone has a different ability to cope depending on many different aspects, including but not limited to their resilience, their perceived level of emotional support, and their ability to reason through situations. People who experience trauma are not weak even if the situation did not traumatize someone else in that same experience. That's what makes trauma so personal.

Trauma changes the way the brain functions, particularly if

the trauma has been prolonged and recurrent. In the book *The Body Keeps Score,* Van Der Kolk (2015) states,

> We now know that trauma compromises the brain area that communicates the physical, embodied feeling of being alive. These changes explain why traumatized individuals become hyper-vigilant to threat at the expense of spontaneously engaging in their day-to-day lives. They also help us understand why traumatized people so often keep repeating the same problems and have such trouble learning from experience. We now know that their behaviors are not the result of moral failings or signs of lack of willpower or bad character—they are caused by actual changes in the brain (p. 3).

Trauma can change the brain so that it becomes difficult for traumatized people to recognize when they are or are not safe. Trauma victims can feel like they're living in a constant state of fear and arousal, and it can be exhausting carrying the shame or terror that accompanies a traumatic event. "For real change to take place, the body needs to learn that the danger has passed and to live in the reality of the present" (Van Der Kolk, 2014, p. 21).

Recently, there have been studies claiming that even ADHD has been misdiagnosed in people who suffer from trauma because of the constant movement of their eyes and the repetitive movement of their hands and feet that is common with flight/flee mode. For example, Dr. Nicole Brown of John Hopkins Hospital who studied whether "inattentive, hyperactive, and impulsive behavior may, in fact, mirror the effects of adversity" has presented her findings which "revealed that children diagnosed with ADHD also experienced markedly higher levels of poverty, divorce, violence, and family substance abuse. Those who endured four or more adverse childhood events were three times more likely to use ADHD medication" (as cited in Ruiz, 2014).

As the brain changes, so do some of its normal functions. For example, brains that have suffered trauma can have a more difficult time with language and understanding communication norms, which can result in miscommunications. Also, regulating emotion can obviously be a challenge as can any kind of executive functioning and higher-order thinking skills as the brain is operating mostly in limbic and reptilian brains. The perception of a trauma victim's world can change as they are more hypervigilant while waiting for the next danger to come to fruition, and normal situations that may not seem dangerous to anyone else may seem threatening to them. The brain also may lose its ability to determine what is reasonable and is not. Therefore, asking a person who is traumatized and has been triggered if their reaction to an event is reasonable is not going to be effective because they may not have the ability to determine whether it is reasonable or not.

Trauma can result in Post-Traumatic Stress Disorder (PTSD), an injury causing deep psychological shock, which can cause changes in the brain that can cause our bodies not to react in the same way that someone without PTSD would. For example, the stress hormones released by a healthy brain to put the body into a survival strategy and then take it out can be hampered. PTSD and traumatized people continue to secrete large amounts of stress hormones, which keeps them in that constant state of arousal and survival.

## BACK TO THE RAGE-FILLED CAR RIDE

The ability to recognize situations for what they are and match words to feelings is one of the first fundamental steps in understanding our own emotions. When we feel disappointment, for example, we are able to step into that emotion, feel it, and attach the word *disappointment* to it, so our brain is better able to define what that emotion is the next time we feel it. From there, we can view the situation to see why we may be feeling disappointment (the trigger), or whatever the emotion might be.

> "Reflection is key to understanding our reactions and emotions and how they're intertwined.
>
> — MANDY FROEHLICH

During the car ride, my son triggered my anger with what he said. My instant, intense fear came from him making a life decision that I believed was a huge mistake, the potential for him to be emotionally engaged with something toxic, and my own motherly fear of watching my child be hurt. My trigger brought on the fight response. I raised my voice, my body was tense and shaking, and for a good portion of the car ride, I don't even remember what I said. I was on angry autopilot. My thinking was nowhere near my prefrontal cortex to be able to think calmly or rationally. The more he would protest against what I was saying, the more escalated I became even though, in essence, he was doing nothing wrong but challenging me. However, in fight mode, a challenge is exactly the way to escalate the situation.

When I arrived home, and we were able to separate ourselves, my brain registered that I was safe and away from the trigger and returned to normal. I was able to think critically about my actions and their consequences and see my son not as a trigger but as my firstborn 20-year-old baby that I had just hurt.

From the standpoint of my own reflection, this is where I was able to say that my anger isn't who I am or who I want to be, so I need help to get to where I need to be. Make no mistake about it, this situation came with all the feels. I was embarrassed, no mortified, that I had not taken care of myself and had allowed my mental health to negatively affect those around me—something I am vehemently against. I felt guilty thinking about what I said to my son, especially in such a critical time in his healing when he was already struggling emotionally. Even writing about it now, I feel tearful and overwhelmed. Though I know that my brain was in a place where I couldn't process what I was doing, saying that out loud feels like I'm trying to excuse my behavior, which perpetuates the guilt. But I'm not. It is what it is.

I apologized to my son twice—once right after it happened and once several months later, when I could tell him everything I had done in counseling to try to heal the issue so it wouldn't happen again. I felt like the word sorry wasn't enough. I needed to prove it with my actions. And with counseling, I have been able to recognize my triggers and avoid getting into that space again. I am not an angry person; I had a moment where I was triggered into being angry. And there's a difference.

> You are not your mental health issue and you are not your mistakes. You are, however, capable of change and responsible for growth and healing.
> You can be resilient.
> You can apologize.
> And you can morph into whoever it is that you want to be.
>
> MANDY FROEHLICH
> #REIGNITETHEFLAMES
> WWW.MANDYFROEHLICH.COM | @FROEHLICHM

## HOW THIS RELATES TO EDUCATOR ENGAGEMENT

The engagement and connection that we feel to our profession are absolutely affected by our current and prior experiences and environment, the way our prior experiences and environments have shaped our brains, and our stress level and the way it is impacting our brain's function, mental health, and physical health. If we are not functioning at near 100% because of personal adversity, professional adversity, demoralization, teacher trauma, secondary traumatic stress, or other mental health issues like depression or anxiety, we may find it difficult to feel fully engaged in the profession that we consider to be our calling. Below are some examples of how this might look:

***Scenario One***

Growing up, an educator struggled to find their place in groups and often found themselves to be submissive and to lack self-confidence (Paleo-Limbic system development). Their trust in others was low. Therefore, working with other professionals including their direct colleagues and instructional coaches, administrators, and support personnel is a struggle because they fear other people's judgments and being ostracized (trigger), which keeps them from seeking out collegial support and growing a professional learning network (avoiding the fear). Their colleagues push to get in the teacher's classroom to help, support, and implement necessary district initiatives, but the teacher, unable to see how they fit into groups, resists. This creates negative relationships (professional adversity) and more avoidance (survival strategy - flight/flee). When they begin to disengage, they lack the support that they desperately need because they weren't able to cultivate it from the beginning and subsequently feel more ostracized and alone inducing chronic stress and further disengagement.

***Scenario Two***

A teacher who grew up with a volatile, bipolar mother who was often abusive (trauma) is assigned a student who is regularly explosive and physical (teacher trauma). The educator is not given time to cope with or process the violent situations, as they are expected to go back to teaching the rest of their students. The constant fear of expected violence activates their PTSD. Even though their PTSD brings on hyper-vigilance, anxiety, and depression (other mental health issues), the educator continues to work with the student and empathize with their home situation, which causes the teacher to also develop secondary traumatic stress. The physical and emotional toll causes the teacher to take sick days to stay in bed and try to sleep it off, increasing the isolation and guilt that the teacher feels from being away. The chronic stress they already feel from their PTSD is increased, and sickness begins to affect their home life (personal adversity) and induce disengagement.

***Scenario Three***

A newly-graduated administrator is excited to get into their new school to make all the changes they dreamt of when they were a teacher (Neo-Limbic brain - hopes, motivations), but they are unsure they "have what it takes" to do to change the negative climate/culture that is in the school they've been assigned (Paleo-Limbic brain development - self-confidence). Their fear is that they will not be able to coach the strong personalities of the teachers in the school and will look incompetent. In the first semester, the teachers refuse to do most of what the principal asks, and the principal sees little change, which seems to solidify their thinking that the teachers couldn't do the job in the first place. The trigger of feeling incompetent (trigger) causes the principal to overcompensate by implementing strict compliance measures to try to force change (professional adversity). This not only causes stress for the principal, but for the teachers as well, and contributes to the negative climate and culture in which the principal was trying to change in the beginning.

Lucky for us humans, the beauty of understanding all of this is that we have the ability to change it. We have the choice to learn, reflect, and engage. We have influence over others who may need the support to do the same thing. Now that we know the what and the how of disengagement, we can take a look at what can be done to move forward and re-engage or stay engaged.

# II

# ENGAGEMENT

It's okay if you don't know what to feel, if you don't know what you want and if you can't figure things out as you go. It's okay to not want something you worked so hard on getting—after realizing it wasn't what you thought it was. It's okay to change your mind, to make mistakes, to walk away from someone you once loved - from something that once meant the world to you. It's okay, because this is your life, your cause, your body, your beliefs, your mind, your heart, and your feelings. And you don't need validation from no one, other than you, and I hope it doesn't take you a lifetime to realize that.

— R.M. DRAKE

# 4

## THE TIES THAT BIND

### DEVELOPING PURPOSE AND CORE BELIEFS

I've never flown in a hot air balloon. The thought of being in nothing but a wooden basket high up in the air held together with a few ropes and a thin, stitched piece of cloth that is a few feet from a burning flame has always *flipped my hey, this could end in disaster* switch. The fact is, I know what happens to hot air balloons in cartoons. We've seen it countless times. A big gust of wind comes, and all of a sudden, the adorably-dressed, talking animal is thrown out of the basket and somehow lands on the top of the balloon, which gets a hole and crashes into the nearby mountaintop. The cartoon character always seems to make the wrong decision, trying to patch the hole with their pants instead of dealing with the fact that they're clearly headed toward disaster.

For me, in this scenario, what may be an even greater fear than mountaintop or my own mortality would be the one of not having control over what was happening. The unknown of what to do if a big gust of wind came and I didn't know how to steer or if I turned up the helium a little bit too high, and the thin material that was the only thing holding me in the air instantly went up in flames. There isn't even an illusion of control. And in the face of this kind of situation, all I would be hoping for was the rope that tethered me to the ground: something to provide that semblance of control where I could pull myself to safety no matter how much the balloon was flailing about and threatening to crash.

Many of us have these virtual tethers in different areas of our lives—people, traditions, lineage that makes us feel grounded and connected in some respect. They may look different depending on our background or stories. Some people have strong ties to family, which allows them to feel grounded. For others, these ties aren't as strong, and they have created their tethers with people who are not blood-related, but connected by strong feelings of friendship and love. These tethers keep us from floating away or facing adversity alone during a big storm. For those of us who recognize our tethers and value them, we also recognize when others don't have them. Those people seem to float through different aspects of their lives with no direction, and when it comes to adversity, they get lost in the struggle with nothing to grab onto.

I don't believe that we all have tethers in every aspect of our lives and that when we are missing the anchoring ropes that hold us down, we are more likely to float haphazardly in the air. I think that in some areas, we feel more grounded than others. The power of tethers comes from recognizing where they are presently, and where there are ropes missing which need to either be created or reinforced. There needs to be purposeful work done to create the tether. When you feel grounded, steady, and in control, it becomes easier to work on building your platform or purpose, developing your core beliefs, and understanding what drives you and knowing what you stand for.

Core beliefs are the tenets by which I keep myself tethered to education because they are the ideas and rules that help keep me grounded. By developing my deep reflection skills, I was able to determine what I consider to be my core beliefs. I only realized that I was even doing this after I had written on my blog for a while and noticed some patterns in my own thinking. It took time and a great deal of practice. I can now rattle these beliefs off at any point, and I bounce every decision I make off of them. Developing these beliefs has also made me more engaged in my profession. I know what I stand for. It is incredibly powerful to understand what it is that makes you tick and holds you up when it comes to certain ideas and concepts in education, especially in the face of adversity. There are times when these beliefs are my lifeline and assure me that I am making the right decisions when they align with these philosophies. I am also more bound to my thinking when I write about it and put it out there for the world to see. Similar to writing down actionable goals, I feel like if I want to be who I say I am, I need to live the ideas that I write on my blog.

If tethering ropes keep you steady, then knowing your purpose is what anchors you to the ground. When I ask people what their purpose is, they typically respond with something like, "to teach my students how to be (good people, smart, social studies experts, hard-working…)," but a purpose is more than that. It is the existential question of "why are you in education (purpose) and what change, specifically, is your passion?" Your purpose is your reason for being. Imagine having a why so powerful that it's the driving force behind everything you do.

In my fifth year of teaching when I disengaged, I realized the only thing that was keeping me in education was the salary. And not that the salary was that great (and the insurance was getting worse by the year), but I had to pay my bills and feed my own children and needed the money. I couldn't take the chance that I would quit and lose even the money I was making. I felt under-qualified to do any other type of job. While other companies seemed to appreciate that I could teach (or train), in their eyes, I didn't have the background necessary to understand the content of what they needed to be trained. Also, part of the issue was me being inside my own head. "I hate my job and I'm not good at this," is not the type of self-talk that makes you want to get out of bed in the morning.

At home, I believed I knew my purpose - it was being a mom. So much of my identity was wrapped up in motherhood that I had no idea who I was as an individual anymore. For example, when I was younger, I loved riding horses more than anything. Years later, until my young daughter mentioned one day that she wanted a pony, I had forgotten that entirely. How can you just forget something entirely that was so important to how you define yourself at one point in your life?

The most dreaded question that I get asked in a podcast interview is, "What do you do for fun?" For years I had no idea how to answer this question. A few times, I actually thought about lying and just inventing a fun piece of me that wasn't actually there, just because it seemed so ridiculous that I wouldn't have a single activity that I would consider a hobby. One time during a podcast interview, the host asked me how I relax. I told them I take my work outside.

I. Take. My. Work. Outside. "In the sun," I said, like somehow that made the answer more viable.

*Um, yeah.*

While some people might say that being a mom is what keeps me grounded and it should be enough, as my children have begun moving on to college and my role in their life has shifted, finding out who I am has become even more important. There's no football practice or baseball games or parent-teacher conferences anymore to fill the hole I've created where my identity used to be. Certain roles might keep us from flying away, but knowing who we are, and our purpose is what keeps us grounded.

Many educators I know have molded their entire identity around education as well. I know this because I have, too. I take care of my own kids and go to their activities, and I work, and that's it. For years that's what I've done. And no matter how proactive I was in those spaces—keeping track of appointments and calendars for the kids, planning and implementation of projects at work—I always felt behind in everything I did and had way too much on my plate. I was trying so hard to be proactive in a very reactive, untethered life, and the effect was a total inability to feel like I was ever caught up.

There are negative feelings that accompany the feeling of being behind: anxiety, nervousness, irritation, and disruption of sleep cycles, making you tired, which adds to the negative emotions. If you're perpetually feeling this way, it's going to affect your relationships and interactions both personally and professionally. This was the way I was, and feeling behind and untethered contributed to my disengagement from education. If I was going to re-engage, I needed to find a way that I could combat these feelings because it's difficult to want to stay in a profession that is so emotionally charged when you feel no emotion towards it.

As I saw it, when I made it my mission to re-engage, I had several areas to address. These were my early realizations:

1. The re-engagement was on me, which was the most important realization I came to. Many times when I say this, people say, "But if my administrator..." I get it. I have worked with those people, too, and it is tough. But the hard truth is that your administrator, no matter how bad or amazing they are, is not responsible for your engagement. Ultimately, it is yours. If they are contributing to your disengagement, part of re-engaging might possibly be a change in location. I have had to make this choice. However, my recommendation is to first evaluate what is happening from the lens of an outsider. Sometimes, we get so far down a path of dislike or uncooperative behavior with each other that everything seems catastrophic, and it's difficult to look through a more rational lens. But, no administrator, colleague, parent, student, board member, or paraprofessional is responsible for your re-engagement. The sooner that someone understands this huge responsibility, the sooner they can begin the journey to healing. For me, if I was going to re-engage and try to love my job again, the decision and effort had to be mine. I spent a great deal of time blaming

everyone else for my issues. It was time that I took control of my own emotions and how I view myself within situations and stop being reactive and frankly, super-negative.

2. The fact that I was reactive was one of the reasons I was always feeling behind. The other reason was that I was taking on every project and opportunity that came my way because I had no direction or purpose. Therefore, I was overworking myself for what felt like very little return, which felt frustrating and would cause me to be more negative.
3. Because I was working so hard and didn't have extra time, the first thing that went was my own self-care. I thought it was frivolous, and people who exercised or went for massages were wusses. Clearly, I was so much tougher and hardworking than them because I could go without those things. I was so, so wrong. That feeling of self-importance and invincibility was one of the first things that needed to go.
4. I needed a lifeline, and it couldn't be something external that could disappear. While my relationships with colleagues and students needed to be part of the solution, I needed a tether that I would carry with me wherever I went. Something that if I left a grade-level, role, building, or even district that I would have it. I couldn't rely on an external tether that I may need to leave behind that would devastate me and my re-engagement process. I needed to discover my purpose,

and with that, hone in on my core beliefs that would support that purpose.

## PURPOSE AND CORE BELIEFS

As part of my re-engagement challenges that I set out for myself, I began blogging. At the height of my disengagement, I switched roles and districts and found I still hated my job. As part of the technology integration role I had taken, I was sent to a conference where George Couros was keynoting, and we chatted. Like he does with many people, he challenged me to start blogging, which I thought was ridiculous, but I started, and I found that I didn't want to stop. I'll follow up with more of how that worked for me in an upcoming chapter.

After a year of blogging, I looked back on my entries. I started to see trends in my writing. I looked at the blogs of other educators that I respected, and noticed that some people had a different focus than I did. Without really realizing it, I had been developing my core beliefs all along.

After working with my core beliefs over an extended period of time, I realized that I had an overarching belief. I called it my platform until I read Deanna Singh, author of *Purposeful Hustle: Direct Your Life's Work Toward Making a Positive Impact* (2018). In her book, Singh defines your purpose as definition, and the work that you do to follow your purpose, your "hustle," and I realized that over time I had created a tether that was internally focused and which tied me to education. My purpose is the tight rope that holds me to everything I do. I can recite it at any time, and I believe it with all my teacher's heart and learning soul: I support educators because I believe that when we support educators, we best support our students. It makes me happy just typing it because, for me, it fills me up with intention, reason, and pride. I'm many things; an educator, a leader, a coach, a student, a learner...but no matter which role I'm filling today, my purpose never changes. It is the reason I'm here. It's the reason I write this book.

Believing in a more specific or specialized purpose isn't exclusionary. I don't believe that students shouldn't be supported just because I support educators. I don't believe that other stakeholders should be ignored because I focus on them, either. I have created a focus that I believe has far-reaching implications. My passion and drive come from understanding that within the ecosystem of education where students are always the focus, we can't sacrifice everyone else at this expense. Like any ecosystem, if one piece of the system is failing, the whole environment will fail. I'm choosing to focus on an area that is traditionally forgotten, knowing that in providing this support, I am working to keep the whole system healthy.

My purpose may not be yours. You may not agree with my purpose. Both are okay. What makes my purpose so impactful for me is that I know I believe it so fully that I don't need anyone else to agree with me. I don't need validation here. That's how I know it's truly mine.

Developing core beliefs and a purpose in itself is taking a proactive approach. You are setting yourself up for understanding how everything you do in a day and every idea or project that is thrown your way can be chosen. One of the reasons I always felt behind was because I was taking every opportunity that came my way, regardless if that opportunity was helping someone else meet their goals or if it was helping me meet mine. I was frustrated because I was all over the place, and many times I found that the projects I took on did not actually support the direction I wanted to go and didn't help meet goals. Not that you shouldn't take on opportunities that help someone else, but there needs to be a symbiotic relationship—a give and take. If you're in a space where 99% of what you do either doesn't live within your purpose, follow your core beliefs, or is for someone else, you're going to feel stuck every single time because you are absolutely spinning your wheels and getting nowhere. You'll not only be stuck professionally, but the frustration will continue to take you down the path of disengagement.

If you get to the point where you've discovered your purpose and core beliefs, it'll feel like you know exactly what you stand for, and most of the time, where you're going...it's amazing. But, honestly, there's no better way to have your beliefs tested than to have them challenged. It's incredibly uncomfortable to have your teacher's heart attached to these beliefs, and then have an administrator or colleague ask you to participate in an idea or initiative that goes against them. If you really believe what you've stated, these beliefs and your purpose are a part of you, and having them challenged means that to participate in the activity will be similar to giving up a part of yourself.

At its root, it's demoralization. It's like saying *everything that I worked so hard to determine didn't mean as much to me as I thought.* If you really immerse yourself in these beliefs and what you need to do goes completely against them, it can make you feel like a caged animal. At one point in my career, I had to leave a district without a job lined up in order to live according to my professional purpose. I can't describe the amount of stress and sadness I felt as I walked out on the amazing teachers who relied on me for support, but because what was happening in the district actually went against my purpose in helping them. For my own mental and physical health, emotional well-being, and to live within my purpose, I had to leave. Because when you live truly within your purpose, and you're in a situation that consistently battles that purpose, there feels like no other choice but to leave and pray that the next placement supports your purpose and core beliefs, and luckily for me, it did.

That all being said, I found that in having the purpose and core beliefs, I needed to develop more of an open mind and evaluate the initiatives that were being handed to me. I couldn't just say, "I'm not doing this because it goes against my core beliefs," without hardcore evidence as to why it truly won't work. I would probably have been spoken to (or reprimanded) by administration for making unapproved adjustments in the areas I didn't agree with if I didn't open communication. Because I had flushed out my core beliefs, I was generally able to give solid reasons and researched-based evidence as to why any tweaks were necessary. The other option was to look at the initiative through a different lens. Occasionally, an initiative that didn't seem reasonable when looking at the outcomes could actually fit into the purpose or core beliefs box, even if the way we were told to get there rubbed me the wrong way.

Discovering your purpose and core beliefs is paramount to re-engaging or staying engaged when circumstances seem tough, and you need a lifeline. There are several steps I took to develop my purpose and core beliefs.

***One: I reflected through my blog***

I looked at my reflections and found themes in my writing. More about blogging will be in an upcoming chapter; the reflection doesn't need to be in this format. It can be in video blogs, journals, sketchnotes...but it should be in a tangible format so you can review it after some time. "Keeping thoughts in your head" or jotting down one-liners won't be enough. It needs to be an activity that forces deep thinking and reflection. Also, keeping it in your head will just clutter it up, and if you're anything like me, you need all the space up there you can get.

***Two: I developed a professional learning network (PLN)***

I wanted to know what other people thought, and I wanted people to challenge my thinking. I needed new ideas. I needed someone to tell me I was on the right track. I needed to read things I didn't agree with in order to understand what did resonate. This process is often enhanced by knowing what you wouldn't do or agree with, along with what you would. Negative situations still teach us what spaces we don't want to be in. I also needed to put my ideas out there that followed my core beliefs. I needed people to challenge me, so when my beliefs were challenged in my presence and practice, I already had a plan of how to react (again, being proactive).

***Three: I created my own professional learning opportunities***

I read books, watched webinars, attended conferences and Edcamps, and took online courses in passion areas. For many of the same reasons as I developed a PLN, I also participated in activities that would give me higher access to thoughts and ideas. It was paramount in helping me grow.

***Four: I developed stronger connections***

I focused on positive relationships. I found a group of people outside my district who could identify with my celebrations and struggles with no judgment and enough of a distance that their suggestions could come from a completely sterile place with no prejudgments because they weren't in the same building or district I was in. Sometimes, I needed these people to tell me I was wrong. As we tend to affiliate ourselves in our buildings with like-minded individuals who will egg us on if we get irritated, I needed people in my life who would tell me I was out of line and give me suggestions on how I could handle situations better. These were my people.

***Five: I looked for opportunities that would satisfy my purpose***

Living within your purpose means running every project idea or opportunity through the lens of your purpose and deciding whether to take it on. This is one of the ways I began to rid myself of the feeling of being behind. I found that a majority of what I was doing didn't actually support my purpose or my own personal goals, and I had to learn to say no. I also found that there were projects that I really wanted to do that I had to let go because they didn't fit there either. I knew that any time that I spent on activities that weren't aligned to my core beliefs was time I wasn't spending on ones that are. I found that when I aligned my activities to my purpose, I not only felt more fulfilled, but I grew exponentially. I didn't feel stuck. Instead, I consistently felt like I was moving forward.

***Six: I paid attention to all the feels***

But I particularly paid attention to anything I did that brought me joy. Then, I did more of that. If it made me happy and fell within my purpose, it tended to be the *"hell yeah"* projects that I wanted more of. The more I did, the more I wanted to do, and the more engaged I was in my work. I also began to pay more attention to activities, people, places, or ideas that caused me stress and began to incorporate more self-care with intention.

## THE RESULTS

When I spent a great deal of time developing, refining, and testing my purpose and core beliefs, this is what I settled on:

Purpose:
I support educators because I know that when I support educators,
I am best supporting students.

Core Beliefs:
Do what's best for all learners.
Teach people what we ask them to do.
Model the behaviors we wish to see.
Start with empathy.
Take responsibility for your professional learning.
Support educators' mental health, too.
Surround yourself with people who make you better.
Focus on purpose.

My core beliefs have been tweaked over time but have not entirely changed. For example, "Focus on purpose" was previously, "Focus on your why," but I later determined that if you are focusing on your purpose, which should be the driver of everything you do, then you are also addressing your why. I have gradually added to them if I find that a strong belief is missing. Another example, "support educator's mental health, too," was my most recently added, a couple of years ago.

Developing purpose and core beliefs is one of the most valuable and necessary components of re-engaging or staying engaged. There needs to be a tether created to hold you, keep you grounded, and make you feel safe. When you know you have something substantial harnessing you and holding you to your calling, you feel less out of control and behind and more likely to pick the activities and battles that help bring you forward instead of holding you back.

# 5

## RE-ENGAGEMENT

Just as disengagement doesn't happen overnight, re-engagement won't either. It is a very personal process...a journey of coming back from an unhappy place, which means the one primarily responsible for determining the steps is the one who is disengaged or on the path to disengagement. In my experience, it can be a one-step-forward and two-steps back turbulent dance where you're unsure of the beat. Making the decision to re-engage can happen in a day, but going through the process takes tenacity, resilience, spirit, and will. The desire to remain in negativity because it's easier will be strong. Things that are worth it are rarely easy.

The steps to re-engagement or staying engaged will be personal and specific to that individual's needs. I also can't say this enough: it is a personal choice to re-engage or stay engaged. One must want it and choose it. And while it might seem like the obvious choice, it's not always obvious to everyone.

The path to re-engagement or staying engaged may also vary depending on the causes of disengagement. Recuperating from burnout, for example, is different than re-moralization. Re-engaging after cancer is different than after a combination of professional adversities. When considering burnout, secondary traumatic stress, and demoralization, however, there are some standard recommendations for healing.

## BURNOUT

The most common medical treatments for burnout are really only to address the symptoms of burnout. Exhaustion, anxiety, and depression are treated even though burnout is recognized as a medical diagnosis. The real treatment is rest, although that's not always 100% possible. Instead, pull back from going one hundred miles an hour by learning to reconfigure your time and how to politely say "no." This is where having a clear purpose will help. If it doesn't fall within your purpose, it doesn't align with what you should be taking on. Even then, however, sometimes alignment doesn't mean it's an automatic yes if we already have too much on our plate. We can help each other out by understanding when someone else says, "I've had enough." One person's breaking point is not necessarily the same as another's.

Another strategy for fighting burnout is going back to basics. Staying hydrated, exercising (even if it's just a short walk), eating healthier, and getting enough sleep can help. These seem obvious, but when I'm stressed, I don't reach for the celery. It's coffee and chocolate and delicious bakery that usually sustains me during these times, which only adds to the issue. Also, think about the last time you got eight hours of sleep. I challenge you to get eight hours of sleep for three weeks in a row and see the difference it makes.

To test to see if burnout is the issue, a reliable, extensive test would be the Maslach Burnout Inventory (educator specific version) developed by Christine Maslach, a leading researcher in burnout. However, this test and the accompanying information book can cost upwards of $50. A simple, free questionnaire can be found on Mindtools.

## SECONDARY TRAUMATIC STRESS (COMPASSION FATIGUE)

The best way to deal with secondary traumatic stress (STS) is to prevent it by educating people on what it looks like. The National Child Traumatic Stress Network, an advocate for the support of professionals who serve children who have suffered trauma, has identified the following concepts as essential for creating a trauma-informed system that will adequately address secondary traumatic stress. Specifically, the trauma-informed system must:

- Recognize the impact of secondary trauma on the workforce.
- Recognize that exposure to trauma is a risk of the job of serving traumatized children and families.
- Understand that trauma can shape the culture of organizations in the same way that trauma shapes the world view of individuals.
- Understand that a traumatized organization is less likely to effectively identify its clients' past trauma or mitigate or prevent future trauma.
- Develop the capacity to translate trauma-related knowledge into meaningful action, policy, and improvements in practices.

These elements should be integrated into direct services,

programs, policies, and procedures, staff development and training, and other activities directed at secondary traumatic stress. (National Child Traumatic Stress Network, 2011)

Many of the trauma-related committees that I've been a part of have focused on student trauma, but a system built with fidelity will focus on educators as well.

When prevention is too late, and someone is already showing the symptoms of STS, mindfulness techniques and self-care have been shown to help, especially if there is an element of group participation for accountability purposes and the social aspect of healing. Sometimes, it is necessary to be seen by a professional either through an Employee Assistance Program or a licensed therapist. The idea with STS is to get to a point where you understand where your role begins and ends with students, and to have the emotional capacity to let go of things you cannot control. According to Secondary Traumatic Stress: Self-Care Issues for Clinicians, Researchers, and Educators (Figley, 1999), STS is beginning to heal when "...caregivers are satisfied with their ability to help the client, there is an understanding as to where the caregiver's responsibilities end and the client's responsibilities begin." Part of loving your students is being able to be your best self for them, and that may include separating your emotions enough to avoid getting secondary traumatic stress.

## DEMORALIZATION

Demoralization is different from other issues, and because it is not widely recognized, it may be overlooked as something that needs to be addressed with specific strategies. For example, while

I believe that we should all be practicing micro-resilience and increasing our coping skills, resilience is actually not an issue with demoralization. Addressing resilience may help with burnout or STS, but demoralization is when the moral standards an educator has is being challenged. It is not that they are unable to cope with what is happening; it is that they feel like what is being asked of them is against their moral code. This has nothing to do with resilience, yet in many cases, we harp on resilience as one of the ways to "fix" disengagement.

Demoralization often has to do with educators not feeling like their voices are heard. Therefore, actions and activities that allow voice, showcase identity, and recognize who you are and what you stand for will fly in the face of demoralization. Blogging or podcasting, becoming an activist for a cause you believe in, taking a stand against something that is against your moral code, understanding your identity as an educator, and what you bring to the table - these are all ways to re-moralize.

Another strategy for re-moralization is to connect with people and groups that provide opportunities for growth. In *Demoralized,* Santoro (2018) states, "For many of the teachers I have interviewed, connections with professors and university programs contributed significantly to their professional longevity. These collaborations provided teachers who were experiencing demoralization ways to enact their moral centers that felt meaningful and impactful." These same experiences can be had through connections with a professional learning network. Also, finding your purpose and core beliefs can support this process by aiding you in understanding that what you do is meaningful and impactful every single day.

As I've stated previously, re-engagement or staying engaged is not an easy trek. Determining if your feelings are demoralization, burnout, or secondary traumatic stress is just one piece of the puzzle to put together. Maybe none of them fit, and that's okay. There are more ways to address re-engagement or staying engaged. Because engagement is intensely personal, the strategies that I used to re-engage might not be what works for others. However, at least giving them a try is a great start. Five strategies I used to re-engage were:

1. Understood the ways disengagement happens and how to get back (already discussed)
2. Reviewed and renewed my relationships
3. Learned to authentically reflect through blogging
4. Discovered and focused in on my passion area
5. Celebrated quick wins and little joys.

## REVIEWED AND RENEWED MY RELATIONSHIPS

Relationships in education are enormously important. When I re-engaged and took a closer look at the relationships I had cultivated, I wasn't happy with how they operated. There was a lot of competition and sarcasm, backstabbing and negativity. It made me feel terrible and only added to the constant stress I was feeling. I knew my approach needed to change.

As I've grown and worked with more and more people, I've realized that I have a knack for creating quick, deep relationships with people. I didn't know I was doing it at first. People would tell me that they felt such a connection to me, and I thought it was just because I was friendly. My closer friends would actually ask me how I do it. They didn't understand why people would reach out to me that I really didn't know very well and talk to me like we had been close-knit friends in another life. They wanted those kinds of relationships, too. "I'm super funny," I'd tell them. They'd vehemently disagree and want to know the real answer. As I've paid more attention to the things that I do both when I work with people in districts and my PLN, I've noticed that there are certain characteristics of relationship building that create deeper connections than just being friendly.

When we address the engagement of educators, there will always be a piece of engagement that has to do with how people feel about the relationships around them. People stay in an organization for the people. You become loyal when the relationships with your colleagues are strong. When we discuss self-care or the need for additional support due to burnout, demoralization, or secondary traumatic stress, there is a need for caring, supportive relationships with people who understand our profession. These relationships need to be built before we need them, so they are in place and a foundation of support.

### *What types of relationships are there?*

Your professional learning network (PLN) is the people that you connect with, both inside your buildings and virtually, who support your goals and aspirations. Sarah Thomas coined the term PLF for Professional Learning Family, which, to me, is a subset of PLN. Your professional learning family supports you both personally and professionally, and you have tighter relationships with these people than you do your PLN. Beyond that, I also have a smaller group of friends that developed out of my PLN that are more like the family in conjunction with the professional. While we talk about professional topics, we are able to switch from professional to personal and back again easily without issue. They are like my sisters and brothers. I lean on them for support, and while some days they might drive me crazy, I would go to bat for them at any point for any reason without even being asked.

There are also different purposes for relationships, and that's okay. I have people I'm close to that I know I can have a serious conversation with. I have my go-to people that I need when I'm having an anxiety attack. There are a few people that make me smile just by hearing their voices. Sometimes I need people who can support me through a tough time, and sometimes I need people to help me celebrate an accomplishment. They can be the same people, but sometimes they're not. Different relationships have different purposes.

### *What does support mean?*

My favorite definition of support is: to bear the weight of something; hold up. Overall, this is what your PLN does for you. However, support can look a few different ways. It can be the need for someone to vent to when things get hard without needing advice. It can be collaborative in nature, maybe when a risk fails, and you need someone to help you figure out where you went wrong before you try it again. It can also be when we have a celebration and just want someone to tell us "congratulations" and validate the hard work we are putting into our goals. It can also be holding someone up when adversity strikes, and they don't know how to get through, and the feeling of giving up is the most attractive option.

***Do I really need to love everyone?***

Education really is such a strange profession. In any other job, you may not be asked to create relationships where there is a great deal of emotion involved; however, in education, everything we do is based on emotion: love of learning, love of kids, love of relationships. And while I'm definitely not suggesting you fall in love with your co-workers, there is a level of emotional stress that requires someone who understands how we feel. There is a type of connection that comes with that understanding that is unique.

I also don't believe that you need to be best friends with all your co-workers, but instead in a caring professional relationship. Even if your personalities do not typically jive, the best cultures in a school are partially based on the educators understanding that they have each other's backs. This includes administration as well -- going both ways. The teachers need to believe that the administrator has their back, but the administrator should feel the same from the staff.

## FIVE WAYS TO CREATE SUPPORTIVE RELATIONSHIPS

### *Be Consistent*

It's not about the extravagant showings, but rather of the consistent way you show someone you care that matters. Someone who positively shows consistency is typically reliable, and they do the things they say they're going to do when they say they're going to do them. As human beings crave routine and reliability, a consistent person feels safe. Of course, I'm speaking of the ways we can be positively consistent. Someone can also be consistently late, consistently a complainer, or consistently do hurtful things, but those are not the kind of consistency that breeds healthy, supportive relationships.

### *Be Vulnerable*

I am a person who naturally shares my vulnerability. I believe this comes from being extremely empathetic, almost to my own detriment sometimes. When I feel like someone is struggling, I will share my own struggles. This does a few things: (1) It models that vulnerability is accepted between myself and the other person: (2) It represents me extending trust to the other person and hoping for a safe space: and (3) It communicates that not only am I not perfect, but I know I'm not perfect. When I have shared vulnerabilities with others, I have noticed the look of relief as the acknowledgment that they're not alone spreads across their face. In one simple gesture, I have created a connection that will be remembered. While the moment may pass with the person not reciprocating the openness, I believe it plants a seed, and the connection is there regardless.

### *Be Available*

When I was a teacher, I was fortunate to have two principals who had a true open-door policy. The only time the door was closed was if there was a private conversation or a child was melting down. I would waltz in their office with needs that, in the grand scheme of things, could have been put in an email. If I was honest, it was more about the fact that I needed adult interaction after being with 10-year-olds all day, and I was using the adults for that purpose. When I became a Tech Director, I tried to model this same availability and noticed right away how difficult it was to get back into what you were doing after you were interrupted. I reflected on my principals and how often I did it to them, and marveled at how they never seemed rattled when I walked in. If they ever had acted that way, I may have been turned off and not gone to them when it really mattered. Part of being available means that you make time even when it's inconvenient. If you're walking down the hall and you ask how someone is, you better be ready to stop and listen.

### *Be Non-Judgmental*

It is very difficult (but possible) to be non-judgmental all the time. Our judgments are based on our biases and assumptions, and if we are not constantly checking them, they get in the way of our relationships. When you compound that with our desire for everyone to be doing the best job they can for students and that our profession entails giving feedback, it's easy to slip into judging based only on the information we have. Being intentional with mindfulness practices will help if you struggle with being non-judgmental.

When we are judgmental, the perception is that we feel we are better than whoever we are judging. The fact is that the negativity really starts within us, and we are spreading it like a disease to others. Instead, a better option is to seek to understand why someone is the way they are or why they do what they do. Even with this information, you still may not understand it: however, you can make a more informed decision as to if there is a way to help or how you can be more respectful of their decisions. I've found that as I've gotten better at this, I've been able to let go of a lot of animosity and irritation about things that, in the long run, never really mattered.

### *Be the Person You'd Like to Talk To*

Be open. Be kind. Say things like, "What can I do to help you," or "I'm so sorry that's happening," or "That is incredible! I'm so happy for you!" Think about what you need when you're celebrating or your struggling and be the person that you'd want to have next to you. You never know when you're going to be the difference-maker for someone or if you're the only person they have to go to. Always assume that they've come to you for a reason. One day, it's possible you might need the favor returned.

There may be times when you don't get along with someone, or you have a disagreement (or 20), or you feel like all they do is complain, and you can only take so much of their negativity. But, it's imperative for the sake of our professional engagement and modeling healthy relationships for our students that we make an effort to have caring professional relationships. Creating these kinds of relationships isn't always easy. There are times when people reach out to me when it's not convenient, or maybe I'm having a bad day, and I honestly don't know if I can listen to someone else's bad day. But, I do it anyway, and I muster everything I've got to provide them with that support. And that is one of the major differences between people who create deeper relationships. The moment you choose to do it anyway means you're invested. It's about making sure that the people around us (both in-person and virtually) feel supported and know that there is always someone who has their back.

## LEARNED TO AUTHENTICALLY REFLECT THROUGH BLOGGING

Learning to authentically reflect would be one of the hallmark changes that need to happen to re-engage because you can't change what you're not willing to recognize is there. It took me until I was an adult to figure out how to deeply and authentically reflect. Nobody taught me how to do it, and the only reason I know now is that I made it a mission to discover what deep reflection could do for me. Deep reflection is also one of the five characteristics of a divergent teacher that Elisabeth Bostwick and I developed, which states,

> Divergent teachers recognize that significant growth cannot happen without taking time for deep reflection. They know how they reflect best, whether it's through writing, meditating, or driving quietly in their car on the way home. They have strategies in place to allow them to take the time and hold reflection in high regard as one of the reasons they are who they are professionally. Deep reflection goes beyond what could go differently in a recent lesson. It also leads an educator down the path of discovering how their own beliefs and assumptions affect what they do in the classroom or how they perceive and communicate with others. Understanding the difference between surface-level reflection and deep reflection is an integral part of divergent thought. Once you understand what you believe, how it affects what you do and how you are perceived, it is easier to change your behavior and push yourself forward (Froehlich, 2018).

So often, we regard the question, "How could things have gone differently/better?" as the be-all and end-all of reflective thought. It's a fine place to start but does not necessarily lead us down a path of reflection that will end with how our involvement affected the ending. It still gives us the room to blame other people or things for anything that may have gone wrong. Deep reflection begins with questions that force us to think deeper about a situation. In paying attention to my own reflective thinking, I've developed five questions to help guide reflection to be deeper than the typical surface-level thinking. There may just be one of these questions used or a few, but the result will be our discovery of adjustments or changes we can make within ourselves to change the trajectory of similar situations moving forward.

***Is there something in my own personal or professional journey that is creating an assumption or bias?***

There has been special attention brought to how our journeys and personal stories affect the way we act, believe, and teach. I am 100% in support of that being the case (as shown by the topics in my book *The Fire Within*). After all, it's our differences that make us stronger together. However, it's also our journeys that have embedded certain assumptions and biases into our thinking. It is nearly impossible to operate completely without them, but it is important that we recognize if there are internal drivers for decisions we make and the interactions we have that may be negatively affecting them. Recognizing assumptions and biases and opening ourselves up to testing them in favor of finding alternative ways of handling situations will move us to more effective decision-making. It will also help us recognize places where our own negative thinking is impacting our day to day emotions. Finally, the recognition of areas where we need to address those assumptions and biases may make us more positive individuals.

***Are my expectations appropriate?***

This reflection path will most likely be followed up with additional questions that can range from logistical (*Have I provided them with the professional learning opportunities they need to do what I'm asking them to do?*) to spiritual (*Is there something in their past/current situation that makes this change/decision/action difficult and they may need more emotional support?*). In order to answer these questions completely, you may need to gather additional information and return to the reflection. Another question that would fit into this category: *Do I have the right to have my expectation of this person, or should it be up to them to set their own expectations upon themselves?* If we are setting up inappropriate expectations and then getting disappointed when someone else doesn't meet them, it can contribute to our feelings of failure and impact our positive relationships.

***What could I have adjusted to create a possible alternative ending?***

Some states have a "no-fault" rule if you are in a motor vehicle accident. If you have gotten rear-ended, you are still partially at fault. Why? How could this be when you were just sitting there waiting for the light or parked legally minding your own business? Because you were there. Because had you not been in that spot, the accident wouldn't have happened. Every situation that we reflect on is similar to this concept. We have had a part in the outcome. Sometimes, it's something major that affects relationships, breaks trust, or perpetuates a negative feeling. Sometimes it's as little as an unintended initial reaction or facial expression. There is always something that we can adjust in order to adapt to any situation and possibly change the ending. Deep reflection allows us to see these things and create an alternative ending when it happens again in the future.

***Do I have something to apologize for?***

A friend once told me, "I don't like to apologize because it's hard." But I feel like if it's really that difficult, that usually means it's the right thing to do. Something being hard should never stop us from doing the right thing, and sometimes that means swallowing our pride and apologizing. An important follow-up question is: *Am I really sorry, or am I just saying it to move on?* Also, just saying, "I'm sorry," really isn't enough. When the apology isn't specific, it loses some of its power. It needs to be truly authentic, and the added specificity will help the person know that you've given it thought, and you know where you went wrong.

If you just apologize just to satisfy someone or move past a bad situation, people will know. I have actually said these words: "I'm sorry that I made a decision that didn't make sense to you at the time. Not only did I allow other situations around me to influence the decision that affected you, but I didn't give you the information you needed to see why I was making the decision. For all that, I am sorry."

Also, just because you reflect and process and decide an

apology is necessary, don't forget that the person you're apologizing to may need additional time to reflect and process the apology depending on the severity of the situation. Be reflective enough to understand that just because you've decided to say you're sorry doesn't mean that the other person is ready to accept it.

***What did I do that went really right?***

Deep reflection doesn't always mean we are looking for ways we have screwed up. It's just as important to remember and celebrate what went well so we can replicate it if similar situations come up in the future. If we never celebrate the great things we do, we will live with the anxiety that nothing we ever do is right, and that's certainly not true of anyone. As we discussed previously, if we live in the gloom and doom, our brains will rewire to expect that. The trick is to find the balance between recognizing what went right and what could be adjusted to find our areas for growth while still remaining positive about what we accomplish.

True, deep reflection is a skill that needs to be practiced. Some people do it during quiet, alone time, and some need to write it down to work through it. It's not always a fun process, as we are looking for ways we can improve or situations we may have negatively impacted, but the amount of personal and professional growth that can be experienced is exceedingly rewarding. Few other activities can have such a lasting impact on how our relationships function and our decision-making process.

## BLOGGING

As mentioned earlier, there are many ways to reflect. I chose to reflect in the form of blog posts because it was the only way I knew how to at the time. Now I also create videos and podcasts, but honestly, blogging challenges me the most because I am not a natural writer. I need to work really hard at writing, and because it takes me so much time and energy to reason through how to write something down so it makes sense, blogging is the best for me. Just to be clear, I blog because it's the most challenging for me, not because it's the easiest; it's just the best way for me to reflect. I am also not super-intelligent, I am not full of ideas, and I am always busy. I don't say this to be self-deprecating. I say it because these are the reasons people always give me for not taking on a project like a blog or podcast. I am relatively normal, just like everyone else. I just choose to challenge myself because I know it's good for me.

I have already made it clear that I have used my blog to develop my purpose and core beliefs. By watching for themes in my writing, I was able to determine what I truly believed and what held me up. I was able to determine my passions and understand what I brought to the table. Remember, it is incredibly powerful to understand what it is that makes you tick and holds you up when it comes to certain ideas and concepts in education, especially in the face of adversity. There are times when these beliefs are my lifeline and assure me that I am making the right decisions when they align with these philosophies. I am also more bound to my thinking when I write about it and put it out there for the world to see. Similar to writing down actionable goals, I feel like if I want to be who I say I am, I need to live the ideas that I write on my blog.

I also blog to give back to my PLN. I often felt like I was taking from my PLN and not giving back. Even though this isn't the reason I blog, it is a great side effect. People often miss that a PLN is a community of learners, and in order to receive, you need to give. While I never expect my PLN to read it, I do feel like even if one person a week reads a post along with my interactions on Twitter, I am at least contributing to my PLN community. It has also allowed me to grow my PLN and make deeper connections as people feel like they can get to know me through my blog posts and I through theirs.

Probably the main reason I blog besides the authentic reflection is that I can create space in my head. If I am turning something over in my mind, trying to reason through it, blogging forces me to get it written down. I need to make it a coherent thought in order to share it out, and that takes a significant amount of working through the issue before I can do that. Once I have done this, I can stop thinking about it chaotically in my head, and therefore, create some space. This is something I developed over time as I practiced effective reflection and putting my thoughts into writing. Creating headspace also contributes to my mental health and has been what keeps me blogging.

While I have focused on blogging, this same idea works for podcasting, vlogging (video blogging), or if it is kept personal, journaling. As long as the element of reflection is present and there can be themes found within the content to develop core beliefs and purpose, it would still fit the bill of what blogging did for me.

## DISCOVERED AND FOCUSED IN ON MY PASSION AREA

Even prior to discovering my core beliefs and my purpose, I knew that I needed to find my passion again. Similarly to how I had lost myself and my interests personally, I wasn't really sure what drove me professionally. Originally, I got into teaching for that lightbulb moment for students, and as I worked through my blog and attending Edcamps and conferences, reading, and connecting with people, I found that I actually enjoyed that same concept with adults—the lightbulb moment when they understand what's being asked of them and they can apply it to help their students. I loved that. Luckily for me, I was already working in a position as an instructional coach where I could explore that further.

The only way that I came to this conclusion, though, was trying new experiences and discovering what it was that I was drawn to and what I didn't enjoy anymore. It meant that I put myself into situations where I was often uncomfortable. I attended Edcamps where I didn't know anyone and had to sit by myself. I started presenting at conferences even though my palms would sweat, and I'd spend the entire session feeling like I was going to hurl because of my fear of public speaking. If I wanted my situation to change, I needed to take myself out of my comfort zone instead of continuing to do the same things and expecting different results.

## CELEBRATED QUICK WINS AND LITTLE JOYS

Finally, another strategy I used to re-engage was to learn to create meaningful goals for myself, break them into quick wins, and recognize the little joys that I had in my life. Previously, the only goals I ever had were either forced onto me by the district where I had no real empowerment in creating the goal or were huge, long-term goals like finishing a degree. I rarely created a goal that I really wanted to meet because I was so entranced by what I wanted to learn that I was excited to get through the steps in order to meet the goal. However, that was what diving into educator mental health did for me.

When I realized that my passion was helping educators, that my purpose was supporting educators because I knew when I did, I was best supporting students, and when I went outside my comfort zone and shared vulnerability with people and watched their response, that was the moment when I dove into the issues of burnout and mental health and was completely engrossed in what I was doing. Those goals were mine. The quick wins of learning something new and applying it was completely driven by me. I became personally empowered, and the joy that I experienced from that was where the magic of engagement happened.

## GOAL ACTIVITY: BEGIN YOUR JOURNEY

No matter where you fall on the engagement continuum, there is always work to be done. Whether you're completely feeling disengaged or you'd consider yourself an engaged educator, moving forward is important for everyone. My challenge is for you to declare a goal that stirs you up and makes you want to go full steam ahead. Something that you need to hold yourself back from working on right now. From there, break the goal into little wins. Put the smaller goals on the calendar, and no matter how tiny or how silly, celebrate them. Tweet them out, do a little dance, text your best friend. Whatever makes you happy, do that. Then take a moment to bask in the joy of that little win, and then look forward to the next time you get to celebrate. Those positive feelings will begin to grow and spread. That's the feeling of engagement.

6

# OUR BRAINS AND BODIES ON POSITIVITY

When I was growing up, the culture of my family was deeply rooted in negativity and sarcasm. Sometimes, the sarcasm was the funny kind that really didn't hurt anyone (more like irony). But there were many times that jokes were made at the expense of others. It was how they "showed their love," and as I got older, I spent a great deal of my young adult life deciding if that was how I wanted to live as well. While I didn't subscribe to the thinking that I needed to put someone else down as a way to show my love, I absolutely did live in a very negative world for a long time. People found my sarcasm funny, and even to this day, I have a difficult time letting go of that part of my personality.

When I began to build my PLN, I began to meet people who were perpetually sweet and kind and positive. It drove me absolutely nuts. Their positivity actually made me uncomfortable, and I didn't like the way it made me feel...at first. At first, I couldn't name the uncomfortable feeling, but it started to grow on me, and one day, I realized that I didn't want to feel those negative feelings anymore. It was like quitting smoking cold turkey. I just didn't want it. I realized that the uncomfortable feeling I felt was a sort of contentment and...light that I had never felt before. As uncomfortable as it was, I wanted more of that.

I spent years wiring my brain, unintentionally, to be negative and sarcastic. I have now spent years trying to rewire my brain to be more positive. It's a struggle, and most days, I still find my sarcastic humor creeping in. But I have come such a long way, and now the uncomfortable feeling comes when I'm around negative people too long. Now, the discomfort has to do with a kind of feeling I don't want, of negativity, and that's how I know I'm changing.

As with many pieces of what people typically consider to be their personality—habits, mindfulness, positivity and gratitude, purpose—if you've been doing them one way for a period of time and then want to change, it will take time to rewire your brain. Again, the brain learns what you've done the most and will want to continue to do it. It takes intention and effort to make those changes. Similar to making the decision to re-engage or stay engaged, this is a choice. Once you make that choice and start doing more of it, your brain will follow along.

## MINDFULNESS

Particularly concerning trauma, self-awareness is one of the ways we recognize emotions and the way our bodies feel and create understanding of those sensations. Mindfulness, as discussed previously, has two major elements: awareness and attention. Jon Kabat-Zinn describes mindfulness as, "One way to think of this process of transformation is to think of mindfulness as a lens, taking scattered and reactive energies of your mind and focusing them into a coherent source of energy for living, for problem-solving, for healing" (as cited in Van Der Kolk, 2015, p. 209).

Practicing mindfulness calms down your sympathetic nervous system, so you are less likely to be thrown into a survival strategy. It has been shown to have a positive effect on depression, anxiety, and chronic pain. Studies have also found that it activates the brain regions involved in emotional regulation and can lead to changes in body awareness and fear, making it less likely to react to triggers (Van Der Kolk, 2015).

Dr. Ashley Anne, founder of Lotus Healing, integrative medicine doctor and licensed counselor, tells me that there are three ways to deal with emotion: feel, share, act. **You must feel the emotion, you must share it with someone else (remember, we are by nature social creatures), and then you must act on it.** She is often telling me to "step into the emotion" and then to name it. In order to feel the emotion and name it, you must be able to be self-aware enough to recognize it for what it is. Mindfulness helps with this process. When you know that when your chest tightens in response to fear, you also can recognize that as being afraid, and you know that taking calming breaths will alleviate some of that pressure, you are now learning to cope with that emotion.

## POSITIVITY AND GRATITUDE

Neuroplasticity is our brain's ability to make new connections and rewire. Therefore, when we think more positively or practice gratitude, we are wiring that into our brains. When we feel happy, our brain produces serotonin, which helps us feel "less anxious, more focused, and emotionally stable" (Scaccia, 2017). Thinking positively increases synapse development (areas connecting neurons) in the prefrontal cortex, which improves cognitive function, focus, critical thinking, and creativity. Thinking negatively can actually have the opposite effect, impacting mood and impulse control as well as hindering creativity (Whitaker, 2018).

Practicing gratitude has a similar effect. In order to properly practice gratitude, it cannot be in the form of competition. For example, "I feel grateful because I have a roof over my head, and I know some others don't." Instead, true gratitude focuses on being grateful for what you have or who you are independent of others. Gratitude does not need to be shared to be effective, even though telling someone they're appreciated is still a nice thing to do. Keeping a gratitude journal has been shown to be impactful even in getting better sleep, and a reduction in depression (directly) and anxiety (indirectly; due to better sleep). Practicing gratitude has been found to release dopamine. In *The Grateful Brain,* Korb (2012) states:

> “Gratitude can have such a powerful impact on your life because it engages your brain in a virtuous cycle. Your brain only has so much power to focus its attention. It cannot easily focus on both positive and negative stimuli...On top of that, your brain loves to fall for the confirmation bias, that is, it looks for things that prove what it already believes to be true. And the dopamine reinforces that as well. So once you start seeing things to be grateful for, your brain starts looking for more things to be grateful for. That's how the virtuous cycle gets created.

To train your brain to be more positive, you must first be aware of your own thinking. This is, again, where mindfulness comes in. To change your thoughts, you must be aware of whether they are positive or negative. Here are a few more ways to rewire and retrain for positivity and gratitude:

***Surround Yourself with Positive People***

Your brain has this cute little trick where it will try to copy the people around you. It has what's called mirror neurons, also part of the vagus nerve system (discussed in Chapter 3), and helps us register our social engagement. Their job is to help us be more aware of other people and quickly tell us how we can fit into the “group.” They are the reason we can read a room and know how people are feeling. They are why we will pick up an accent if we move to a new area. They are also the reason that if we are with negative people, we will feel more negative, or on the upside, if we are around positive people, we will be more positive. When I decided that was the route I wanted to go, I began to reduce the amount of time I spent with constantly negative people, which meant that with people I previously had close relationships, I had to make some difficult decisions. I also had to be more intentional with the people I did become close to and look for the positive ones. They are now my people.

### *Make Time to Do Things You Love*

The action itself or the amount of time you spend on it doesn't matter. It just has to be something you love. Take time to recognize the feeling of joy and be grateful that you had the opportunity to participate in that activity. Give it a moment and allow it to fill your cup. I have a friend who loves to cook and the food that comes from it. I have never seen such joy from a person when they talk about food or the special cooking devices he has to work on this hobby. He continually expresses how grateful he is for his ability to make such wonderful dishes and the opportunities that he then has with friends and family when he shares his food. His joy is contagious and makes me happy. Everyone should be able to find that kind of emotion to hold on to.

### *Heal the Past*

One way to move on to more positive pastures is to heal the past.

Holding onto negative emotions only continues to rewire our brains to perpetuate that feeling. While sometimes, for me, it feels like I'm so tired of living some of my past traumas and feelings, I also know that in order to move forward, I sometimes need to look back and heal. Also, going through this process can help develop resilience for the future when adversity may strike again.

Healing from the past can also be related to your professional past and forgiving yourself for disengaging if you've been burnt out or had personal adversity. Healing doesn't always mean personal traumas or past personal adversities. Sometimes, it means forgiving the administrator who didn't support you when you needed it or the bully who made you feel inferior. It may be about recognizing the mistakes you made and letting the guilt go with the intention to do better the next time. Whatever the case, to stay engaged or re-engage, the negativity needs to be dealt with so the positivity has a chance to get through.

## HABITS AND COMPETITIVE NEUROPLASTICITY

Different parts of our brain are responsible for different activities, and the activity and connections that happen in each of those parts is called brain mapping. Brain maps are specific to people and are dependent on how we learn and our experiences and can change depending on what happens to us. When we stop using certain tools or knowledge, our brains will prune that away. Brain maps can also change if there is an area that we need compensation. For example, if someone would become blind, their other four senses would become more robust to compensate.

About 40% of what we do are not conscious decisions but instead are habits. At some point, we decided to do something in some way, and we continued to do it that way. If we didn't have these habits, our brains would be overwhelmed by the input we get and the decisions we make. A habit is the brain's way of conserving energy. When it comes to habits, competitive neuroplasticity is why habits are hard to break. In order to learn a new habit, we need to unlearn an old habit so the new one can take over. We get accustomed to doing what we do when we do it, and it is difficult to override the brain map. Plus, the younger we start a habit, the harder it is to change it, and as we advance in age, our brain maps become increasingly stronger.

When we are trying to start a new habit, the first time we do something requires focus and energy. There will already be a path made, and it will take cognitive effort to override it. Our brain will look to make any path more efficient. This is called myelination, which increases the strength and speed of the message as it jumps connections. This means we need to practice something over and over again to make it stick. The more we fire electrical signals through this connection, the stronger it gets until it becomes automatic. The brain is attempting to expend less energy and make the action more energy efficient.

Remember, the brain cannot tell the difference between good and bad habits. There is no moral judgment. The brain is just trying to be as energy-efficient as possible. Also, all habits stay with us and can come back when we are stressed or drinking or otherwise have less control over our cognitive function.

There are three pieces to habits: 1) the cue or trigger, 2) the routine or action (which can be emotional, physical, mental), and 3) the reward (release of dopamine in our brain). Don't forget that dopamine initiates action. In other words, when dopamine is released, our brain says, "Do that again!" It leads to a craving, which then creates a routine.

When we think of habits, we usually think of exercise or eating healthy, or quitting smoking or drinking. But triggers can bring on emotional reactions as well. Let's use an example of the emotional feels you have on Sunday night when you have school on a Monday. You feel exhausted because it's going to be Monday. You hate Mondays. Everyone hates Mondays. There are literally thousands of memes degrading this ridiculously evil beginning-of-the-work-week day. However, feeling this way is a habit. You haven't even experienced Monday yet to know what it's going to be like, and dreading it before it happens sets you up for a negative day.

To change a habit, first, you must identify the trigger. In this case, the trigger would be knowing you need to go back to work the next day or that you're leaving the comfort of the weekend with your family. Sometimes changing the habit is as easy as avoiding the trigger. But, in this case, even if you call in sick, you can't avoid work forever. Secondly, change the action. Instead of looking at Monday as the day to dread, look at it as the opportunity for the start of a new week. Amazing things can happen on Mondays after people have had a weekend to rest (and make up your own memes). Finally, find a reward. Maybe a reward, in this case, is every Monday that you've been more positive, you'll spend 10 quiet minutes reading a new book after the kids are in bed. Or you'll take a bath or cook a special dinner, if you like to do that kind of thing. Whatever it is, the reward gives you even more to look forward to on that Monday.

Our brains are amazing tools, and knowing that we can rewire them to be more positive is powerful. This rewiring has been shown to work not only in people without mental health issues, but those who suffer from them as well. When it comes to re-engagement or engagement, having a more positive, grateful outlook is a must. When I ask in sessions to describe disengaged educators, "negative" is nearly always at the top of the list. To be engaged, we must have the personal empowerment to take over our feelings and rewire for positivity. This isn't just fluff; it's a real way we have control over our brains and emotions and how our thoughts make us feel.

# 7

## SELF-CARE AND SOCIAL-EMOTIONAL SUPPORT

To be completely honest, while I have been an advocate of self-care for a while, it was more like I believed other people should be doing it, but I "didn't have the time." It wasn't because I valued what other people brought to the table less and felt like I could do better (therefore, they could take time off but I couldn't), I just believed, like many educators, that we want to take care of others but not often practice what we preach. I found that even when I would plan to practice self-care that I would ultimately cancel it or cut it short to adjust for other people's needs. I was consistently the first person that I would break my promises to, which was a blatant disregard of my own self-worth, and frankly, my health.

It was only when I began to feel the pull of burnout, symptoms recognizable because I had been there before, that I started to look at self-care as "preventative medicine." If I wanted to be my best and at the top of my game in both my personal and professional life, the answer was not working myself to death. Instead, I needed to allow my brain and body to rest so they could be working at a higher frequency and I could be more productive, instead of working at 50% and accomplishing my to-do list but in a half-assed fashion.

If I was going to "do" self-care, I first needed to find out what I even liked to do. Because I had lost so much of what made me an individual when I threw myself into motherhood and my profession, I really had no idea what I would even enjoy. I was embarrassed to admit it. I grew up in a household where doing anything for yourself was seen as selfish and unnecessary. Getting your nails done, massages, taking a break, praying…these were the activities of the rich and snobby. "We" didn't do them. Instead, any activity of self-care was replaced with multiple glasses of boxed wine from the refrigerator. I not only needed to figure out what I liked, but I also had to fight against the ingrained idea that "extras" such as these are frivolous and the guilt that accompanies the feeling of acting in selfishness.

> "As we grow up, we gradually learn to take care of ourselves, both physically and emotionally, but we get our first lessons in self-care from the way that we are cared *for.*"
>
> — (VAN DER KOLK, 2015, P. 110)

The definition of self-care is taking an active, intentional role in your own well-being and happiness. Self-care needs to be practiced daily to be the most effective during times of stress. The most integral part of that definition is the intentionality that must go into self-care. Many times I hear people exclaim the need to begin to pay more attention to themselves when stress is high, and it usually accompanies something like, "When everything calms down, I'm going to learn to (insert a commonly quoted self-care activity)." However, if self-care is figured out early and practiced with more regularity, it will be a routine in times of stress that will lower your body's response to that stress. It's more difficult to get into the flow of a self-care routine when you're already all out of whack.

You're still saying, "Ok, I get that, but I'm really just too busy." I see you, friend, and I recognize your type because it's also mine.

I have a podcast called Teacher's Aid through the BAM! Radio Network. Every show is closed with the familiar phrase, "Put your own mask on before helping others," in reference to what the flight attendants say you're supposed to do if your flight is in trouble. When I first started flying with my own children, I would look at them and think, "How could you ever sit and watch them struggle while you put your own mask on first?" It seemed like the ultimate trade-in of my mom card to help myself before helping my kids or anyone else I cared about for that matter. This mentality is similar to why we often neglect what we need in favor of others. We will give every ounce we have to help anyone else before helping ourselves. What we often miss about this is that the more we give, the less energy we have to do anything right. If I put my own mask on first, I could get all four of my kids' masks on quickly after that. If I put one or two masks on first and then pass out, I'm no longer able to help my other children. (That sounds dramatic, but you get the idea.)

Taking care of ourselves is exactly how we give our best to others. When we keep our cups full, we have more to pour from. Self-care is how we refill our cups. So, when you start to realize that, you start to understand how truly unselfish it is to practice self-care.

## THE GREAT SELF-CARE DILEMMA

As we begin to focus more on mental health, the advice to practice self-care is popping up more often. Articles and other resources give advice on activities such as practicing relaxing, yoga, and mindfulness or meditation. But the first step we miss is to find the thing that works for that individual person. It may or may not be meditation or yoga, but it should be the thing that makes a person feel like themself and calms their soul. But what happens if you don't know what that is?

There are a few aspects of self-care that make it difficult to practice. First, self-care can't be done for you. Unfortunately, self-care at its core is about bringing you back to feeling like you, and you are the only one who can do that. It's that fleeting feeling you get when you've settled into a moment, and it feels like home. Nobody can do that for you.

Second, it's difficult working in a profession where our entire efficacy is wrapped up in how someone else is doing, yet we need to move from focusing on them to focusing on us.

Third, we don't know what to do. This is especially the case if it has been a significant amount of time since we have taken a moment for ourselves. We forget. Like, literally, we have no idea where to start.

While I do seriously enjoy working in education, I've also come to realize that just because you love what you're doing doesn't mean it won't burn you out. Balance is key. Too much of a good thing is still too much. But even knowing this doesn't mean that I know what to do to relax. By spending so much of my life going and moving and working, I have trained my body to be unaccustomed to focusing on things that help me unwind. I have also forgotten what makes me feel like myself outside of education. I can tell you my core beliefs and what my passions are inside of education. Outside (beyond caring for my own kids)... no idea. I'd try to watch TV and quickly get bored, and my mind would float back to all the things I had to do for work. I'd make it ten minutes before picking up my computer. I felt agitated and out of sorts when I tried to do anything else because I wasn't enjoying what I was doing more than working. Then the cycle would continue.

So this idea of self-care for me has not been fixed by learning yoga or practicing meditation. I don't like yoga. My body doesn't want to contort that way. And meditation is a work in progress. I'm still at the point where being completely inside my own head makes me uncomfortable, but because I believe it's important, I'm trying to see if it's for me. Discovery of who I am outside of education has been a journey of trying to remember who I was before I was a teacher and activities I would try that could be considered self-care. I first reflected on the things I used to do that I enjoyed when I had more balance in my life. Everything either didn't fit into my current lifestyle (horseback riding, for example), or I didn't enjoy it any longer (watching movies). I realized through this journey that I had lost what made my soul happy and needed to find it again. The question became:

> How do you practice self-care when you've forgotten what makes you feel like you?
>
> — MANDY FROEHLICH

While we quickly try to solve the self-care dilemma by telling people common areas to focus on...exercise or meditation being the most common, this is not the first step to self-care. If we believe that yoga and meditating are the only ways to practice self-care, and that's not what makes us happy, then we are less likely to take care of ourselves like we need to. These things may work for some people, and that is awesome. But in order to enjoy them, it needs to be a part of that person and what they enjoy. The first part of the journey in developing self-care is rediscovering who you are and what you like, which can require so much more reflection than it seems like it would. It can feel like a dark place when you realize that you may need to find yourself again. Giving yourself permission to recognize that what works for you may not be the same as what works for someone else, and giving yourself grace as you search, fail, and search again will help you find the self-care activity that keeps you engaged, impassioned, and whole.

### FIVE GUIDELINES FOR SELF-CARE

#### SELF-CARE FEELS GOOD AND MAKES YOU HAPPY

Focus on positive self-talk
Avoid drama and negativity
Let go of what you can't control;
focus on what you can
Know when to say no
and be excited about saying yes

## SELF-CARE ACTIVITY: STEP ONE

Before I introduce the four types of self-care, take a piece of paper and write down everything you do that you would consider being self-care. Anything you can think of. Keep the list close, as we will be revisiting it before the end of the chapter.

## TYPES OF SELF-CARE

My first goal was to do research, and I found that people had lists of different types of self-care. Sometimes, the types numbered between ten and fifteen and always with the message, "you should be doing all of them." It was overwhelming. How did it make sense to have so many types of self-care to pay attention to, that your self-care in itself was stressful? I read through the lists and consolidated it down to four types of self-care that seemed to encompass all the important areas. Four types I could handle.

There was no way I was remembering more than that, especially when I was stressed and needed it most.

***Physical Self-Care (Take Care of Your Body)***

Physical self-care is how you take care of your body. Many people insert exercise here, and moving your body, raising your heart rate, and keeping yourself limber are all great examples of physical self-care. However, physical self-care also involves what you put into your body. Eating healthy and taking vitamins can affect how the body functions and reacts to sickness. Drinking enough water and staying hydrated is imperative. Dehydration, vitamin deficiencies, or being low in vitamins such as Vitamin D or Iron have been linked to depression. Also, physical self-care involves going to the doctor not only when you're sick but also for preventative measures. It means taking care of yourself and resting if you're not well.

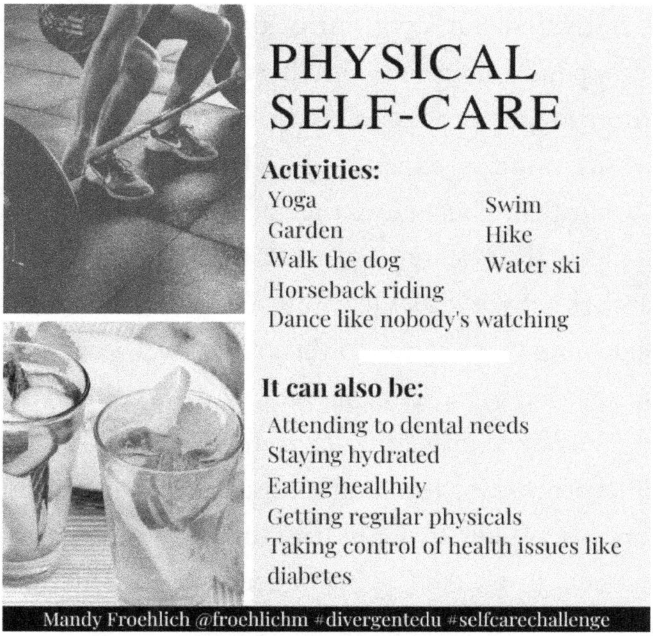

PHYSICAL
SELF-CARE
Activities:
Yoga
Garden
Walk the dog
Horseback riding
Dance like nobody's watching
Swim
Hike
Water ski
It can also be:
Attending to dental needs
Staying hydrated
Eating healthily
Getting regular physicals
Taking control of health issues like
diabetes
Mandy Froehlich @froehlichm #divergentedu #selfcarechallenge


Physical self-care ideas in five minutes or less:

- Complete a short workout on an app like Workout Trainer
- Stretch
- Do jumping jacks
- Complete a lap around the classroom/school/house
- Park further away from the store

***Intellectual Self-Care (Take Care of Your Mind)***

Typically, when I do my workshops on educator mental health and engagement, intellectual self-care is the type reported to be most practiced by educators. We are natural learners, and if we have cultivated our own curiosity, we continue to want to learn and expand our minds. Intellectual self-care is expanding your brain, thought processes, and personal growth. When you feel like your mind is expanding and you are thinking deeper about a topic that you enjoy, that activity would probably fall under intellectual self-care.

Research is showing that learning a new skill can also slow the cognitive decline from aging. In the article *Back to school: Learning a new skill can slow cognitive aging research has shown that exercising the brain is similar to exercising the body* (Solan, 2016), the author states. "The process of learning and acquiring new information and experiences, like through structured classes, can stimulate (new brain cell growth)." The brain needs new challenges to keep it healthy.

Practicing intellectual self-care is not about just learning something new. When we do so, we are actually causing physiological changes that keep our brain functioning at a younger age.

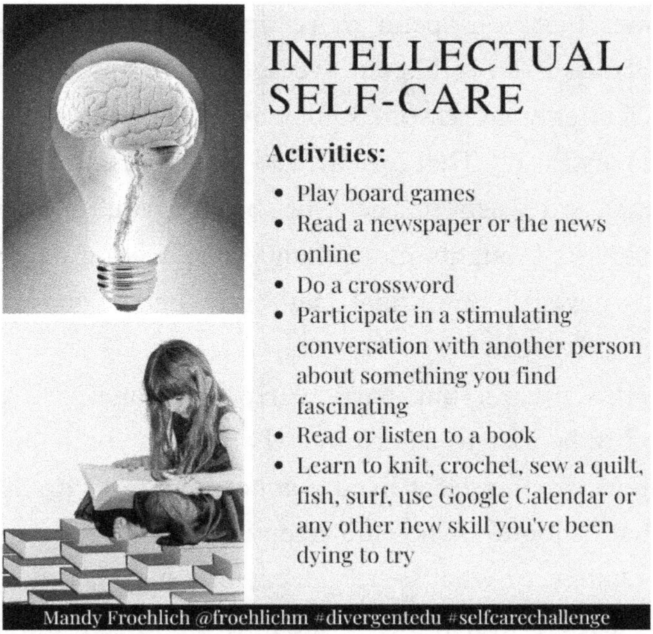

INTELLECTUAL SELF-CARE
Activities:
• Play board games
• Read a newspaper or the news online
• Do a crossword
• Participate in a stimulating conversation with another person about something you find fascinating
• Read or listen to a book
• Learn to knit, crochet, sew a quilt, fish, surf, use Google Calendar or any other new skill you've been dying to try
Mandy Froehlich @froehlichm #divergentedu #selfcarechallenge


Intellectual self-care ideas in five minutes or less

- Watch a YouTube video explaining how to do something you want to know
- Research directions or best practices for a project you want to try
- Read a blog post
- Listen to a podcast (or part of a podcast)

***Emotional Self-Care (Find Your Balance)***

Emotional self-care includes activities that help you feel balanced. Balanced does not mean 50/50 all the time. Even if your life is balanced, there will still be times you work more and other times that you spend more time with your family than work. Balance is more like an average. Some days you will feel sad for seemingly no reason. Some days will be happy, and some might be frustrating. That is okay, and it's important to recognize that balance and accept it. The issues begin if you're feeling negative feelings or thoughts more than you're feeling happy for an extended period. Emotional self-care helps guard against becoming imbalanced.

For all self-care, but particularly emotional self-care, it's important to be able to determine what makes you happy, joyful, and content. For myself, I lived a good portion of my life doing things that "should" make me happy, or what others told me made me happy, or what society deemed as happy. When I began to focus back on myself, one of the most important questions I'd ask when I started practicing self-care was to see if I even *enjoyed* what I was doing. Sometimes, that answer was no, and I needed to rediscover what was going to fill that hole. This kind of self-reflection partnered with trial and error is okay. It will help you find what will sustain you.

EMOTIONAL SELF-CARE
Activities:
• See a counselor (appropriate even when you're not struggling)
• Keep a journal
• Spend time with friends who build you up and make you laugh
• Learn to accept a compliment
• Practice positive self-talk and being kind to yourself
• Learn to recognize your stress triggers
• Lay in the sun
• Practice forgiveness
Mandy Froehlich @froehlichm #divergentedu #selfcarechallenge


Emotional self-care can also involve activities that will help you take a proactive approach to reduce stress. For example, developing a sustainable budget for your family, decluttering your home, or discovering a better way to organize your time can alleviate stress when an outside source is throwing you off. Having pieces of your life put in place like this will take the burden of them off your plate when the rest of your life is stressful.

Another often overlooked part of emotional self-care involves letting toxic situations, people, and things in your life go, which means reflecting on your choices and how others are affecting your well-being, and possibly making difficult decisions that may at first make you feel unhappy. In the long run, however, it results in better overall happiness in your life. Also, practicing positive self-talk and recognizing your worth and what you bring to the table is all part of emotional self-care.

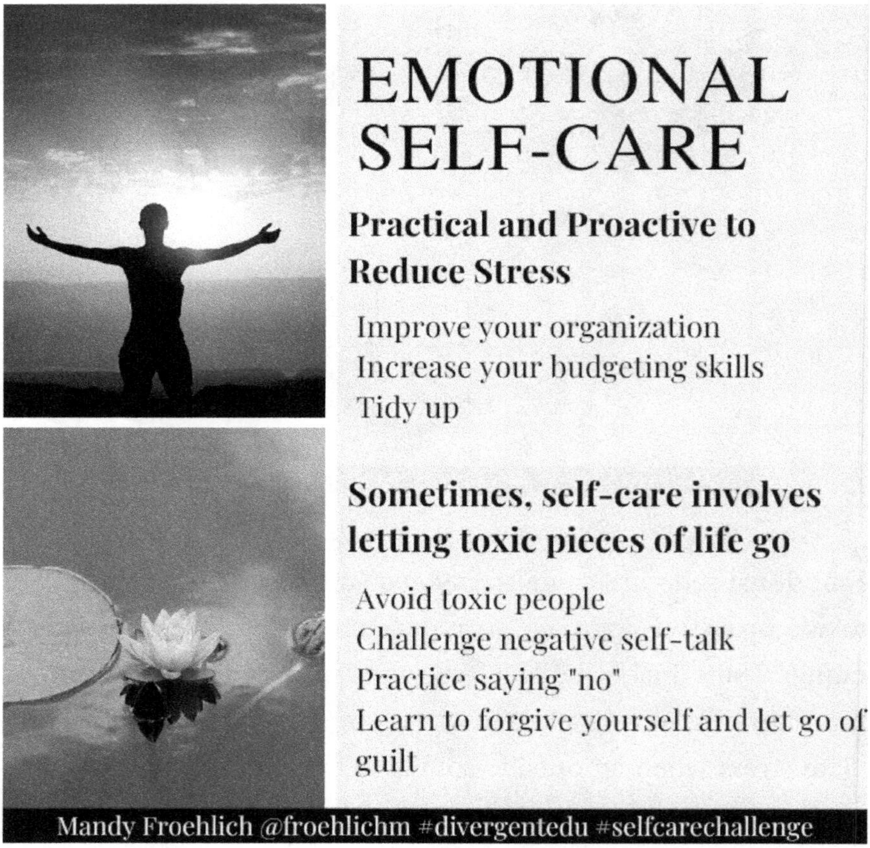

EMOTIONAL SELF-CARE
Practical and Proactive to Reduce Stress
Improve your organization
Increase your budgeting skills
Tidy up
Sometimes, self-care involves letting toxic pieces of life go
Avoid toxic people
Challenge negative self-talk
Practice saying "no"
Learn to forgive yourself and let go of guilt
Mandy Froehlich @froehlichm #divergentedu #selfcarechallenge


Emotional Self-Care Activities that Take Five Minutes or Less

- Listen to your favorite song
- Cuddle with your pet
- Take a five-minute break from whatever you're doing
- Slow your breathing
- Light your favorite candle and enjoy the aroma

- Tell someone you love them
- Give someone a compliment

***Spiritual Self-Care (Find Your Center)***

Spiritual self-care involves anything that you'd do to nourish your soul. Many times these activities overlap with emotional self-care because anything that feeds the soul typically makes you happy and gives you emotional satisfaction. If emotional self-care makes you feel balanced, spiritual self-care helps you feel centered. Self-care in this area can remind us of our purpose or guide us down the path to finding it.

I like to use the analogy of a building. If a building is straight, the structure is sound, and it is "centered," it is more likely to withstand an earthquake. However, if it is off-centered or unstable, any kind of adversity could damage or even level it. We need to protect our foundations and keep ourselves centered on being able to stand the strongest during times of struggle.

When I speak of spiritual self-care in workshops, there are always a few people who say, "I'm not particularly religious, so I'm not good at addressing this area." While some people may use religion and their beliefs as their gateway to spiritual self-care, one does not need to have these same beliefs to practice it.

Whenever I discuss spiritual self-care, I'm always brought back to this story I told once on my blog about the detriment of having a broken spirit:

"I grew up with horses. My horse, Dakota, was a beautiful white Arabian Appaloosa who had been a trail horse after being a barrel racing horse. He was sweet and kind, and I could tie nothing but a rope to his halter and ride him bareback with no issues whatsoever. But we had another horse that was a black Morgan, and she was the most difficult horse we ever owned. She didn't like people, and she didn't listen. She did whatever she wanted and would look at you with the most defiant eyes I've ever seen on an animal. When speaking to a friend about her, she said that she never seemed to really be broke entirely. My horse was always compliant because he was well broke. And I think one could argue that when you break a horse in that you are essentially breaking their wild spirit to get them to do what humans want. Damaging the part of the horse that makes them a horse. Even though she was a rideable horse for an experienced rider that could manage her, she was difficult. But her spirit and relentlessness also caused us to make changes in the barn and the way we did things with the horses that ended up being better practices in the long run. Those things wouldn't have happened if we had completely broken her spirit because the complacent horses would have just kept doing things the way we had them."

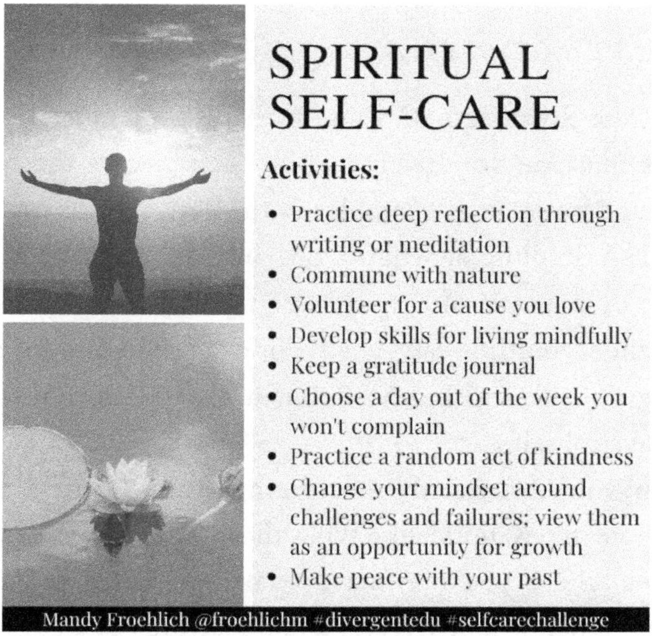

SPIRITUAL SELF-CARE
Activities:
• Practice deep reflection through writing or meditation
• Commune with nature
• Volunteer for a cause you love
• Develop skills for living mindfully
• Keep a gratitude journal
• Choose a day out of the week you won't complain
• Practice a random act of kindness
• Change your mindset around challenges and failures; view them as an opportunity for growth
• Make peace with your past
Mandy Froehlich @froehlichm #divergentedu #selfcarechallenge


Practicing spiritual self-care in five minutes or less

- Send a message to a loved one telling them you love them and appreciate them
- Read a scripture passage
- Thank someone who serves the community like a police officer or crossing guard (or even a fellow teacher!)
- Choose to stay away from gossip (and definitely don't initiate it)
- Send a positive thought or gratitude to someone you may typically struggle with

## SELF-CARE ACTIVITY: STEP TWO

Take out the list of activities you made in Step One. Add in any activities that you do already to practice self-care that you may have missed but read as examples in the descriptions for the four types. Then, looking at what is on your list, mark each activity with one or multiple of the self-care types. Sometimes, self-care can fall under multiple categories. For example, runners often say that they do it to feel balanced, but it also would obviously fall under physical self-care.

When you've finished categorizing your self-care activities into the four types, notice the types that you are already strong in and types where you may need some additional practice. For example, I am constantly reading and learning, so I am strong in the area of intellectual self-care, but I lack practice in spiritual self-care, so I have taken up learning about and practicing mindfulness. Understand that you may need to learn some new skills and create new habits to effectively practice self-care.

## SELF-CARE IN THE CLASSROOM: WHEN BOTH MINUTES AND YOUR PATIENCE COUNT

We all know how it goes. You just need five minutes to give directions. You're one minute in, and you already know you're going to be giving them for a second time to about 30% of your class that's not paying attention. You just came back from walking one student out who was having a meltdown to go take a break with another teacher. You think there might be a fire drill coming up, but you can't remember. As you release the students to work and you go to check your computer for the drill time, three students come up to you and ask about the one direction you repeated three times. And you want to *lose your mind*.

There are times in a classroom when you need quick self-care options that won't throw off your day but will, at the very least, keep your emotions in check and healthy. Here are some suggestions:

### *Take a Deep Breath*

This sounds too good to be true, but taking a deep breath helps you move out of your sympathetic nervous system (fight or flight) to your parasympathetic nervous system (relax). The breath literally tells your body to relax. This is especially helpful if you practice Conscious Breathing techniques, where you are more mindful of how you are breathing. When I would take a deep breath as a teacher, I would couple it with a drink of coffee or water or put candy in my mouth (that was similar enough to a cough drop that I could pass it off). The extra couple seconds I'd get while doing this gave me a moment to focus on my heart rate and breath.

### *Have a Happiness Kit Ready*

I've heard these kits called a few different names like mental health first aid or emotional first aid, but basically, they are the first aid kits for when you need to feel happy. They can be in a small box in your desk drawer and should be filled with small items or photographs that bring you joy. Photos of your loved ones, candy or chocolate, a well-loved memento from a trip, a piece of your security blanket when you were a kid; whatever makes you smile and feel like yourself again. Take something out of the Happiness Kit, put it in your hand, look at it, close your eyes, and allow the feeling it gives you to fill you up. It can only take a minute or two but should provide a feeling of calm before you head back into the trenches.

### *Involve the Students/Have the Students Take a Break*

In the scenario above, the students taking a mental break to regroup and focus back on learning would have been best suited before the directions were given when the teacher knew they were losing them. Taking a break to run through a few easy yoga poses, deep breathing, or even mindfully coloring an easy picture (yes, for secondary, too) for a few minutes in the classroom are all proven ways to get the brain ready to learn. As for the teacher… either using this time to practice along with them or take a few minutes to look at the Happiness Kit will help get the teachers back on track as well.

### *Take Advantage of Therapy Animals*

There are many different schools of thought with therapy animals. How do we balance the value of their use with the fact that some people have serious allergies to them? I understand both sides, and this is not a commentary on whether they should be used or not—it's an endorsement that if you are able to and if they're there, use them. There have been studies showing that therapy animals can have a dramatic impact on anxiety (Brooks, Rushton, Walker, Lovell, & Rogers, 2016). While walking out on your students to find the nearest Golden Retriever is not teacher best practice, it is absolutely appropriate to find the pup when you have an extra minute.

A little planning can go a long way when the minutes count. Understanding what works for you is the first step. Understanding the little things that give you joy is the second step. That takes pre-planning and discovery, but it is information that you need to have to make self-care the most impactful.

## MINDFULNESS

In an effort to understand and practice spiritual self-care better, my weakest self-care area, I became a certified mindfulness practitioner. In the last few years, I feel like mindfulness in schools has become more commonplace, but in many cases, people haven't been trained and don't really know how to effectively implement mindfulness in the classroom. While an entire book could be written on just this topic, I think it's an important part of self-care to at least have a general understanding of what mindfulness is.

Mindfulness is more than quieting your mind. It's more than meditating. Jon Kabat-Zinn, the founder of Mindfulness-Based Stress Reduction, defines mindfulness as "an awareness that arises through paying attention, on purpose, in the present moment, non-judgmentally." He goes on to say, "And then I sometimes add, in the service of self-understanding and wisdom" (as cited in Defining Mindfulness, 2017).

There are two major elements of mindfulness: awareness and attention. *Awareness* is a broader sense of what's occurring in your inner and outer experiences. In other words, what is going on in your environment and what is going on inside your body, including your thoughts and emotions. Being aware of emotions and thoughts can have a dramatic impact on shifting them towards being more positive. *Attention* is channeling your focus onto a particular object or idea and then holding your attention in place for a specific period of time. Meditations are made to do this.

I have been practicing meditation for some time, and I still really struggle with it. At first, I used to joke about my mind being a scary place to be. I felt like I needed to clear out some cobwebs and get rid of some ghosts before I could comfortably sit alone in there. Even still, my mind wanders and depending on the day, I feel like I spend more time bringing myself back to the meditation than I do actually in a meditative state. I can say, however, that successfully completing the meditative practice can be completely day changing. I find I am way more focused and centered when I've done it right. Like exercise or self-care, mindfulness and meditation need to be practiced regularly to be the most effective when stress is high. If you're just beginning, give yourself some grace. If you can meditate for three minutes, then meditate this week for three minutes. Try for four next week. Focus on growth. Over time your brain will come to expect it and settle in faster.

But mindfulness is more than meditation. Before understanding this, I used to think, "I can't meditate, so I can't be mindful." Well, I learned to meditate, but some other important aspects and practices go into mindful practices as well. Some of them feel more concrete than meditation does and are practices that you could start today.

### *Mindful Intentions*

Setting an intention activates your internal guidance system. Setting an intention involves knowing who you want to be and then setting a goal to get there. An intention can be chosen depending on a situation or goal. For example, if communication with a partner is an issue, an intention might be, "I will communicate and listen to my partner without judgment." Then, throughout the day, running any communication through that lens based on the intention and asking, "Am I showing up in this way right now?" If the answer is no, then you know there needs to be a change. Many times we have goals that we are working towards. Setting an intention is like setting micro-goals to help you get there. It is action-orientated. Instead of wishing and hoping that things change or the future gets better, you're making it happen. In the absence of setting intentions, people will continue to operate in the same way.

### *Gratitude Stones*

Gratitude stones are simply a trigger, used positively, to remind us to show gratitude. Gratitude stones are literally stones that you put into your pocket. Every time you reach into your pocket, you will feel the stone, and the idea is to think of something you're grateful for during that time. It's even better if you have the opportunity to write it down.

While I think that the use of an actual stone is intriguing (I imagine a super shiny and smooth one like I used to make in my rock tumbler as a kid), I rarely reach into my pockets. For me, putting a reminder on my lock screen, so I see it whenever I pick up my phone is more effective.

### *Arts Therapy*

Coloring has its place in the practice of mindfulness. Find a picture that has an intricate pattern. A Mandala has a spiritual meaning, but it's the intricacy that is useful for this technique. Any image similar to that will do. The process should take about 10-20 minutes and should be meditative; your focus should be drawn to what you are doing.

### *Body Scans*

For me, one of the most important mindfulness activities to help me deal with my anxiety is body scans. I used to call body scans any time that you were in tune with your body, but there is actually a specific way to do a body scan. I've also found that this same practice helps me fall asleep at night, especially if my mind is racing, and I'm struggling to find sleep.

Body scans can take 10-20 minutes but can last as short or as long as you want. If you have less time, a certain body part or area can be focused on. Notice what it is that you feel or sense without judgment. For example, if there is a slight tightness in your body, try not to label them or judge them as, "this shouldn't be here, I can't wait until this goes away." Just acknowledge it and move on.

Steps for a Body Scan

1. Lay down in a comfortable position.
2. Take several deep breaths in—inhale and exhale slowly.
3. Begin to disengage your mind from busy thoughts or ideas.
4. Gently close your eyes and bring awareness to your body.
5. Notice how your body feels in this moment.
6. Take notice of any intention in your body and where the areas are that are experiencing this tension.
7. Take notice of any areas that are comfortable or relaxed.
8. Bring awareness to the left leg and foot. Notice any sensations - temperature, tingling, etc., and continue

breathing. Become aware of the calf and knee and left thigh. See your breath moving down into your left leg. Allow that leg to become heavier and sink deeper into the floor.

9. Bring awareness to the right leg and foot. Notice any sensations—temperature, tingling, etc. and continue breathing. Become aware of the calf and knee and right thigh. Notice any feelings, sensations, or tightness. See your breath moving down into your right leg. Allow that leg to sink deeper into the floor.
10. Notice your hip area. Notice the sensations. Breathe into the hips and allow them to sink.
11. If your mind starts to wander, notice your thoughts, acknowledge them, and push them aside.
12. Notice your abdomen. Notice sensations and how it moves with each inhale and exhale.
13. Notice your lower back in the same way.
14. Then to your upper back, shoulders, and chest. Pay special attention to any emotions you hold in this area. If anything comes up, notice it, acknowledge it, and then gently let go of any judgments.
15. Notice the sound of your own heartbeat. See if you're able to connect with your heart on a deeper level.
16. Bring awareness to your left arm, hand, fingertips. Notice any sensations in that area. Don't force it.
17. Shift focus to the right arm, hand, fingertips.
18. Guide attention to the neck area. Tension is carried in the upper back and neck. If there's attention, breathe into that area and allow that area to relax. Tell yourself,

"My shoulders and neck are now relaxed and comfortable."

19. Bring awareness to your face. Allow the face to relax and soften. In your mind's eye, allow any tension to be let go.
20. Move your focus to the top of the head. Take notice of how clear your thinking is. Notice how at peace you feel.
21. Stay as long as you'd like, then wake up by wiggling toes, tighten calves and thighs, stretch your arms out and stretch your hands, gently open your eyes.
22. Pause and take notice of the experience. Don't grade it as successful or unsuccessful. Recognize it for what it was.

### *Mindfulness Wrap-up*

One of the reasons I came to love mindfulness so much is the consistent reminder to acknowledge certain thoughts, feelings, or emotions *non-judgmentally*. We are often quick to make judgments about the people and places around us. Especially if we have experienced trauma, making snap judgments can be a fear-based response to trying to keep ourselves safe. It's difficult to feel a pain in your shoulder and not think, "I really need to get that checked out. It could be bad!" But, when I think about how many judgments that I make on a daily basis of people, places, and things that are probably incorrect, I feel like practicing to take the judgment out of my thinking can only be a step towards being a more positive person.

## TECHNOLOGIES THAT SUPPORT SOCIAL-EMOTIONAL CARE

It seems counter-intuitive to find another reason to be on your phone or computer, but the fact is that sometimes we need guidance or help, and technology is one of the best and most efficient ways to get it. It's not using tech in general, but the way we use tech, aimlessly scrolling social media versus using an app to help drive us through a meditation that can determine if it's appropriate for social-emotional support or not.

I've hesitated in the past to name specific apps or technology as it changes so quickly, and that causes this information to cease to be evergreen. However, it seems that when one app closes, another app opens, and just knowing what's potentially available in tech can be helpful.

### *Healthy Habits*

Apps that help build healthy habits are typically specific to whatever habit it's trying to address. Workout apps or diet apps use a variety of methods to keep the user engaged in building the habit, usually with gamification. One app, Fabulous, claims to help build overall healthy habits based on the needs of the user. From its description in the Google Play Store, "Fabulous is a science-based app, incubated in Duke's Behavioral Economics Lab, that will help you build healthy rituals into your life, just like an elite athlete." Categories in the app include areas like *Strengthen Your Self-Control* or *Build Your Exercise Routine.* It takes 21 days to create a habit and 40 days to make a lifestyle change.

### *Mindfulness and Meditation*

There are several apps available that will bring you through a daily meditation, which can be especially helpful if you're just learning. Two popular apps, Calm and Headspace, have offered free educator programs. Their functions are similar, but their user interfaces are a little different. I usually find that people prefer one over the other, but you need to experience them both to decide.

### *Fitness*

If you search fitness apps in any app store, you'll receive thousands of options in return. There will be apps for getting six-pack abs and "a rock hard body in 10 minutes a day." Aaptive and Workout Trainer are apps that guide you through workouts. An interesting app called Zombies, Run! places you in the middle of the inevitable zombie apocalypse where occasionally you may need to run a little faster to escape. If you find exercise to be boring, creative apps like this may be an option.

### *Digital Health*

The newer cell phones usually include an embedded digital health feature. It shows how long you've spent on your phone, how many times you've unlocked it or received notifications, and what apps you spend the most time using. This information can be found in the settings on your device. Another option is the Moment app. The Moment app takes the information a little further, stating in the Google Play Store, "Moment gives you back that time. Through short, daily exercises provided through Moment Coach, we help you use your phone in a healthy way so that you can be present for the parts of life that matter most." In my position as Director of Innovation and Technology, I often worked with students on the use of these tools. A student came to my office one time and said, "Can you please show me how to access that digital wellness information again? The thought that I might be wasting so much time on my phone when I could be doing other things makes me sick." Yep, honey. Me, too.

***Podcasts***

Listening to podcasts can be relaxing for some, but moreover, it can give you information to help support areas of self-care you are working on. For example, if you'd like to get more organized or create a budget, a lifestyle or financial podcast could help you do that. I've been proud to be a co-host on the BAM! Radio Network's Teacher's Aid with Jon Harper. We specifically address strategies for the social-emotional support of educators in 10-15 minute podcasts, which are easily digestible.

# III

# ADVOCACY

You're not stuck. You're just committed to certain patterns of behavior because they helped you in the past. Now those behaviors have become more harmful than helpful. The reason why you can't move forward is because you keep applying an old formula to a new level in your life. Change the formula to get a different result.

— EMILY MAROUTIAN

# 8

## CREATING CULTURES OF SUPPORT

As discussed previously, there is a symbiotic relationship between educator engagement and culture. A supportive culture is one component necessary to keep educators engaged, and engaged educators will contribute to a supportive culture. Every school I have worked with that had a positive climate and a robust culture, without fail, has had over 75% educators (including paraprofessionals and leadership) who I would consider to be positively engaged. *This only makes sense.* Think back to the definition of educator engagement as being, "intentionally seeking purpose and understanding our impact, living within that purpose, and creating opportunities for both ourselves and others to be happier, healthier, and more positively, emotionally engaged people to best serve those around us." Educators feeling like this would lead to a positive and more connected place to work.

Regarding a more innovative culture, when administrators ask me how to empower their staff to be more innovative and divergent thinkers, they're surprised when I often begin with the teachers' engagement. However, I would venture to say that one of the biggest barriers to innovation is how you feel about your job. If I am dealing with any of the reasons for disengagement or have been disengaged for years, my brain is focused and full, and there may not be the capacity for innovative thinking. This reasoning, as I have stated previously, is why educator engagement is part of the climate and culture foundational level in the Hierarchy of Needs for Innovation and Divergent Thinking.

I was working with a district and coaching their teachers in authentic and effective technology integration. The staff was amazing, and from the discussions I had with them, they agreed that they had a strong culture and positive climate. However, in working with one particular teacher who was excited to be there because she hoped it would "help," she admitted that she had volunteered for the pilot technology integration coaching group because she felt like the magic had been lost from her teaching. There had been so many changes over the year, none of them necessarily negative but still a lot, that she felt weighted down and lost. My job there was to help her develop a goal for technology integration, but in order to do that, we first needed to address her downward slope into demoralization because that was the core of the issue. Had I started with technology, it may have been a temporary band-aid if we were lucky, but what she was really missing was recognizing her identity and what made her a darn good teacher in the first place. First, efficacy and remoralization. I believe that when we have re-engagement, the curiosity, innovation, and divergent teaching will come more naturally.

## ADDITIONAL SUPPORT FOR ENGAGEMENT

There is plenty of responsibility to go around when it comes to educator engagement. However, when I speak about disengagement, many people immediately begin looking for something or someone to blame. Blame is only fuel for disengagement. There is a difference between blaming and looking for the impetus, which may be a cause. This transition is the first step in the deep self-reflection and personal empowerment needed to re-engage. It is appropriate to find the cause in order to work on strategies for dealing with that issue. It is not going to help anyone to say, "If so-and-so were more (friendly, competent, organized, punctual, knowledgeable, etc.), then I would be fine." You cannot change so-and-so. And frankly, allowing them to continue to make you unhappy gives them way too much power in your life, anyway.

## COLLEAGUE SUPPORT AND WORK ENVIRONMENT

A few years ago, I was suffering from severe depression and suicidal thoughts. My emotional brain was slowly taking over, telling me I was fat and useless and could never be the person that I was fighting so hard to be. Usually, in these cases, my logical brain takes over and says, "Whoa now, we know that's not true, and we know that's your depression talking, so what can we do to make it through this?" But my emotional brain was so loud it was drowning all logic out. In a moment of clarity, I called to get into a therapist hoping for some help and relief. I looked at our district insurance online and started looking for what would seem like an appropriate psychiatrist. Or a psychologist? Counselor? I wasn't sure where to go. I began calling phone numbers of those listed as "taking new patients" on the insurance website. Call after call, I was told that the insurance was wrong and they were not accepting anyone. Finally, after tens of tries, I reached a receptionist who told me that they had one counselor who was accepting new patients. I quickly looked at our insurance site and found that they were listed, although none of their specialties seemed to fit what I needed. She said that the first appointment they had was three months out. *I may not be here in three months,* I thought.

In desperation, hoping that there may be a quicker emergency type of appointment open, I told her that I was having suicidal thoughts, and she said,

"Are you thinking of killing yourself *today*?"

Honestly. I couldn't make that up.

But, at the time in the state I was in, I thought to myself, *well, am I going to kill myself today*? I knew the outcome of an answer of yes. They would tell me to go into inpatient care. I wasn't ready for the fallout of that. I imagined teachers in the lounge whispering about what happened to Mandy. How she literally went crazy enough to be admitted to a mental facility. At the moment, I felt like I would rather take my chances than to be considered the unstable one, the one who couldn't do her job because she might flip out at any time. The weak one. The one that people would whisper about and tiptoe around. I wasn't ready for that.

I told the receptionist that I was not going to kill myself *that* day and took the appointment three months later. I hung up the phone, not actually knowing if I would be alive to see that doctor. I walked out of my office, plastered a smile on my face, and went about my day as if I hadn't just cried out for help, unsuccessfully.

These types of things are happening in our schools, friends. So, how can we support each other?

## DISTRICT SUPPORT

One of the greatest gifts we can give ourselves and the people around us is to recognize these issues as what they are and create a culture of safety. It is so much more difficult to dislike a colleague when you understand that they may be going through a situation that is causing disruption and possible disengagement. You may speak more kindly to them and may be less likely to think negative thoughts about them. Destigmatizing mental health and the impact of adversity by talking about it is powerful. It creates a safe environment for people to ask for help when they really need it, instead of suffering alone.

It is partially the district's responsibility for cultivating this culture. While individuals need to be open to it as well, the district is in the position of being able to wholly support these efforts. One mistake I see often is the half-hearted attempt of a district to create initiatives that support educators' mental health. In every case, the lack of authenticity shows. Educator mental health is not an initiative. It's a lifestyle. It's not something that starts or ends; it just is and has always been this way. We have just been ignoring it for so long. How you truly feel about it will be apparent in every little message handed down by administration. The district can't, for example, authentically endorse educator self-care and then hand down six new initiatives. On an already full plate, the first item to fall off will be self-care when you have a group of people who traditionally give themselves over to others. Unnecessary compliance measures need to be taken off their plate to make room for self-care, so it is seen as important. Also, what educators are doing for self-care should never be a goal set by an administrator, nor should it ever be a school required goal. Support, yes. Compliance, never.

As I just stated, the culture surrounding mental health will be communicated in every little action a district displays. A great place to start is to truly allow for mental health days for sick leave. This is a tough one during a time where substitute teachers, in some areas, are not always available. However, that mental break will allow educators to come back more focused and productive. Also, understanding that educators need to be able to do what makes them relax on these days is imperative. This may be getting a massage or sitting in the park. They shouldn't be afraid to be seen in public because they need to fake being sick to get a mental break. Communicating this to all staff is an easy step in setting the foundation for supporting self-care and mental health in a more concrete way. Like any business that hires their workers and promises them time off, educators have earned those sick days. Allow them to use them as needed.

Another easy, low-cost option is to have a resource page that is curated with articles, videos, and websites regarding mindfulness, mental health issues, and easy-to-follow steps on finding help through the district insurance. While I understand that everyone receives an exorbitant amount of emails, placing tips in widely read newsletters or even printed out and put on the back of bathroom stall doors can be helpful (for a little light reading while on the toilet).

I understand that professional learning days are few and far between, and there are usually content areas to be focused on. However, providing interactive learning opportunities for school personnel on mindfulness, yoga, doing body scans, self-care, or strategies for dealing with mental health issues for both themselves and their students can be a great way to give them the knowledge they need to help themselves and others. We often ask educators to know how to do these types of activities but don't teach them how to do it, and by the time they get around to it, they are exhausted. Give them contracted time and the resources they need to put them into practice.

One of the most worthwhile implementations would be to have accessible mental health support in the form of counselors that visit the schools and have available times to meet with educators or any other student or adult that may be needing additional help. These types of cooperations with community mental health professionals make it more possible for educators, who are virtually stuck at their jobs non-stop all day, to attend a session when and where it is more convenient for them. This way, they don't need to take a half-day in order to seek help.

## BUILDING-LEVEL SUPPORT

Your building-level team has the potential to be one of the closest work families you have. I've joked that they often mimic those of real families...the eccentric aunt and the hip cousin, the grandmother who is always baking and bringing in treats ruining everyone else's diet. But all these personalities belong to the families, and while we put up with their craziness, we have the capacity to love them as well.

Discussing these topics openly is one way to begin the conversation; however, there needs to be a common understanding of what mental health, burnout, secondary trauma, adversity, and demoralization mean. Many people don't understand, and in that lack of understanding can be harsh or criticizing. We have the power to educate them. *That's what we do for a living.* Start with getting everyone on the same page. Then move onto empathy.

One of my favorite videos is called *Brené Brown on Empathy* and is a cartoon that was created to follow along with one of her keynotes. As in all of Brown's work, she discusses how empathy creates connection, yet we are usually so comfortable in the judgment of both ourselves and others. Sometimes, when another educator is truly disengaged, they can seem crabby and even unbearable, and it is so difficult to show them empathy. It'll take time and effort and consistency, but eventually, that empathy will create the connection that we need to help people come re-engaged and see the light again.

In this same vein, we all need to model vulnerability. If we expect others to be vulnerable, we need to show it. Truly modeling vulnerability is showing someone areas where you need to grow in order to help someone else open up and not feel alone. It will not be done to overshadow someone else's trials or one-up them, and it will not be used in a way to make that person feel like they shouldn't feel bad. When we are truly vulnerable, it is coming from a place of support and understanding.

As part of that family, everyone needs to take responsibility for the truly difficult parts of our jobs and help one another out. For example, there are moments when an administrator, teacher, or paraprofessional is with a student who melts down or becomes volatile. Many times, that student is removed but not without there being, at a minimum, a stressful moment where the educator is trying to calm them down, and it can be escalated all the way until the adult is physically or verbally assaulted. In these cases, there needs to be another person to step into the room after the student has been removed to allow the educator a breather to get their heart rate down, and their nervous system calmed. Their ability to continue the class effectively is going to be hampered anyway, and by not allowing this emotional release, the educators will keep it pent up, therefore, contributing to anxiety and burnout.

We all have a responsibility to support each other when it comes to mental health. It may not be our fault, but it is our responsibility to create an environment of safety and concern when it comes to both ourselves and the people we work with.

# 9

## SWITCHING THE FOCUS

### STUDENT STORIES

When I've spoken about educator mental health, I have often kept conversations of students out of it. It's not to be exclusionary. After all, I believe that in supporting educators, I am, in turn, supporting students. However, in every conversation, I have been a part of, even when I have set out the parameters that we are focusing on educators, it always gets brought back around to students. While it warms my heart that these amazing and selfless people can't seem to talk about themselves, I want educators to understand that it's *okay to prioritize yourself when it comes to your mental health.*

That being said, when I remembered who I was as a teacher, I began to remember who my students were as well, and what brought my passion back was ultimately understanding that the demons I am fighting were being fought by many of them, too. Sometimes, I feel like as adults, we say, "Just wait until you're an adult and you'll have real problems," but I guarantee that many of our students have real problems, some worse than we can even imagine.

This chapter was added in to give a few brave individuals the platform to help us, as educators, understand what is happening within our schools, classrooms, and students that we may feel like we don't understand. I felt myself in some of their stories, and I saw resemblances of some of my own students as well, and they gave me insights into where I could have been a better support when I was just focusing on juggling my classroom.

## MY DAUGHTER'S FIGHT

A morning in August 2016, I was driving to work. Being an administrator, I was wrapped up in getting ready for the beginning of the school year. Teachers and students weren't back yet, but the summer is traditionally the Technology Department's busiest time. I was lost in my own thoughts when I received a text from my eldest daughter.

Cortlynne: *Addie and Goose and I were fighting, and Addie told us she wanted to kill herself. I don't know what to do, Mom. I'm scared.*

I can't begin to go through the emotions that wash through you when, as a parent, you read something like that. I'm going to be completely honest, even though it's going to sound like I'm a terrible parent, but my first thought was that she was being dramatic. My youngest has a flair for the dramatic, and maybe it was wishful thinking, and I thought maybe it wasn't true, and she was just using it to get a rise out of her older brother and sister. It just so happened that my husband was home at the time, and I was so confused as to why she didn't tell him. As I worked an hour away and I was almost to work, a flurry of messaging and calls began.

Me: *Did you tell your dad?*
Cortlynne: *No, I can't find him.*

I messaged my husband, who was in the garage, and immediately went inside with the same disbelief that I was feeling. I called Addie because I wanted to hear how she sounded. She was crying. I asked her about what she said. She told me that she had been thinking about it for about a month and just didn't want to live anymore. I asked her if she was going to do anything right now. I was able to get her to calm down using all the strategies I knew because I often have the same thoughts. In the following days, we had several productive conversations that allowed me to see where her thought process was. It was real. This was no line of drama. No strange way to get back at her siblings. No attention-seeking behavior. She didn't want to live. Nothing made her happy. She felt unsuccessful and hated herself and had thoughts that no 11-year-olds should have to endure.

We also needed to have discussions with our other two children who were living at home because they had been the first to hear Addie's plea for help. They were both nervous, and I think for them, it was a wake-up call as well. I felt it was important for them to hear the basics of Addie's progress and our plans to try to ease their anxiety. Our eldest son was in his first year in college and had missed the conversations, and we brought him in on the situation when we felt we had it under control enough for him not to worry excessively. The impact on our entire family was enormous.

I laid awake at night and couldn't believe the situation I had allowed to happen. I suffer from depression and anxiety, feelings of inadequacy, and a constant underlying current of suicidal thoughts. *How did I miss this?* If there was anyone on this planet equipped to recognize the signs in her own daughter, it should have been me. I should have recognized that she had withdrawn over the summer. She stopped hanging out with her friends as much. She didn't come out of her room as much as she should have. She was quiet, and when she did speak to anyone, she was combative—so much so that sometimes the moments she spent in her room were a relief. I felt like I had allowed this to happen right in front of me, and I was the kind of parent that months prior I would have said, "How could that mom have possibly missed the signs?" I had put our family in a situation where I had to wake up every day praying my daughter would wake up with me. I struggled not to sleep outside her door in case she would decide that she couldn't keep fighting.

With professional help and medication, my daughter has made amazing progress. I tell this story because I missed the signs and almost lost my daughter. I missed her struggle. I missed her depression. I missed her anxiety and obsessive thoughts. Me. Her mom. The one who struggles with her own mental illness. The teacher. The perfect person to see all the signs and help her missed them entirely. Fortunately, the conversations we were able to have were productive because I knew what questions to ask and how to speak with her about her brain and help her reason through her thinking. Our relationship became infinitely closer because of the situation. I'm not happy it happened, but I am grateful that we made it through and came out stronger.

As an educator, I often walk down the halls and see kids doing various things. Some are walking by themselves, heads down, earbuds in clearly trying to block out the world. Some are sitting in alcoves alone and working. Some are happily walking with their friends, laughing, and appear to be successfully getting along with their day. While we may assume that the first two scenarios may present kids with struggles, and they very well might, my daughter's represents another type of person with challenges. She hid her mental health issues very well at school, but the summer downtime had been too much for her to take. When I was in school long ago, I was the same way. I hid my struggles well and instead threw myself into doing well at school, having friends, and enjoying myself while I was there. While Addisyn and I have different reasons for our struggles, they manifested themselves in similar ways. Addisyn is adopted, but this connection we have has just once again reinforced that I was meant to be her mom.

## HOW WE IMPACT STUDENTS

Our students come to school every day with struggles that some of us can't imagine. Their lives are so very different than ours were at that same age as things have changed so much in the last few years, with new innovations and technology, changes in value systems and moral compasses. The way they communicate, collaborate, and interact has shifted so far away from the way we did twenty years ago, yet as adults, because we haven't lived in this shift, it's difficult for us to understand it. Some of us try, but honestly, until we have kids that we either have or are close to going through something difficult, we can't completely comprehend the nuances in situations or specific challenges that they may be facing, let alone try to come up with suggestions that may help. Ironically, we rarely think about asking the kids what they need without trying to "fix" them first. It's usually with the best of intentions: we went into teaching feeling the moral obligation to help children. What we fail to recognize is that sometimes *helping* is simply asking, "What can I do to support you?"

As I discuss in my first book, *The Fire Within,* the increased disengagement of teachers from their professions has a tremendous impact on both our teachers and students. The effect on the teacher is clear. If you disengage from your profession, you are less likely to enjoy what you are doing and put your heart and soul into what you loved about teaching, to begin with: the students. Also, it is more difficult to be connected enough to your students to recognize if they are struggling or to model what engagement in learning and life looks like. After all, if I missed the signs as a mom whose highly invested and connected to her kids, it could happen to anyone, especially if they aren't completely invested in their life's work any longer.

Of course, our impact on students is only one piece of their overall picture. They also have parents with various degrees of parenting styles, expectations, involvement, and experience in raising kids. Some of our students may work multiple jobs in order to help support their families, and frankly, being able to help put food on the table may trump that social studies exam.

## THE INSIDE VS. THE OUTSIDE

I have alluded to my childhood turmoil before in blog posts and go into a bit more detail in *The Fire Within,* but I often keep the details of that experience under wraps. The little bits of information I allow to leak are meant to provide context to my experiences that have made me who I am and, hopefully, help people practice empathy for anyone when you really don't know what they're going through - students or adults. So much of our existence is wrapped up in cycles of joy, contentment, heartbreak, and forgiveness, and sometimes just the act of being normal is a heroic feat of epic proportions.

My family was a prime example of this. From the outside, we were considered to be an exemplary family. We fostered and adopted kids and did respite care. We had a small hobby farm with horses, goats, pigs, foxes, raccoons...even a monkey. The eldest by seven years, I was well-behaved in school, didn't say a lot when I was younger, and I worked hard and received good grades. I could survive in school without a lot of assistance, so I was either praised for my work ethic or ignored completely. I was involved in clubs and extracurriculars. As I got older, we were even recognized as a family of distinction in the city where we lived for all the good we did with foster kids.

At home, we were often on edge. My brother had to wear a dirty diaper on his head because he refused to get potty trained. My sister was told to stand up and hold her nose against the wall for hours for being defiant. Later, in a moment of terrifying creativity, my mother decided to start giving kids shovels and send them out back to dig their own graves. She said nobody would miss them anyway. My mother and stepfather were later arrested on multiple accounts of child trafficking and abuse.

The psychological warfare that exists in abusive homes is the part that I feel we underestimate. My home wasn't always violence and chaos. We had birthday parties and cake fights. We had loads of Christmas presents (even though my mother's compulsion with cleaning wouldn't allow us to play much with them). We laughed sometimes. There is just enough love to suck you back in. To make you think things are ok. That's the kicker. As a kid, you never know when it's going to go south. You just never know. And worse, you can't tell anyone. You absolutely cannot take the chance that you say something and are taken away for two reasons. First, you never know when you'll be sent back and the consequences of that. Secondly, I wanted a family so bad.

It took me until I was an adult to understand that while I wanted a mom, someone who told me they were proud of me and to love me unconditionally, I didn't necessarily want my mom. I couldn't help her enough to fit her into what I needed as a parent, and eventually, to move on with my life, I needed to be okay with that. There was no other way I could forgive.

When I was in high school, I did go to the school counselor and told her just a bit of what was going on. She sent me home because we were such an amazing family that I had to just be making it up. I never made that mistake again. Hide, hide, hide it. Cover it up. Scream into a pillow. Pray.

Recently, I was in a younger classroom where a beautiful soul of a little girl was struggling. She had already left the classroom once, and so I decided to pay special attention to her to try to get her to stay. As I watched her, I noticed she was all over the place. It could have been mistaken as ADHD as she nervously fidgeted and struggled to get her work together, but to me, it screamed trauma and the effects of a constant state of fight/flight. The students were learning how to use a tech tool, and to do that they had to answer questions about themselves just to practice. One of the adults in the room asked this one simple question: "What did you have for dinner last night?"

I have absolutely no idea concerning the background of this student, but I do know what it's like to try to hide what's happening at home. When I looked at her, her face dropped and her brow furrowed. I thought she might bolt, so I made my way to her, and by the time I got there, her head was hung and her eyes were a bit watery. I asked her if maybe she didn't have time to eat the night before and began to silently curse the dinner question in my head. Right before I was going to ask her to change the question to answer for lunch instead, her head popped up and she looked at me with a determined smile, too hard of eyes for a second-grader, and said, "I had pork chops and green beans and mashed potatoes and…and…and…" It's possible that my heart actually broke that day. I felt like saying, *"Oh my little love, you could do great things with that resilience and determination. Just hang on to it a little while longer."* I choke up just thinking about it. Even though I had never gone without dinner—my sister had become a master macaroni and cheese maker—I felt that little girl was me. Struggling to be just normal enough to fit in. Hide, hide, hide it. Cover it up. Scream inside. Pray.

We can say this is a sad story, and we don't want to read stuff like this. That would be irresponsible and negligent to the students who are experiencing it—to our colleagues who have lived through or are living through it.

The lesson here is twofold.

Adversity makes us who we are. We can choose to live in

anger and resentment. Lord knows I have enough reasons to do that. I don't because I choose not to. That means I need to sometimes forgive people who have no intention of saying they're sorry because I don't want to allow them to have that much control in my life. That also means I can use what I learned in the classroom with students and hopefully give them the support they need.

Our students are going through things that some of us can't imagine. Look at them. It would have been easier to get irritated with her for bolting from the room. It would have felt reasonable to send her to the principal when she blew up because nobody knew how a question like that would trigger her. But, she's a child. A little kid. And worth our time, attention, and love.

As my work has turned to be more with educators and I have been diligently supporting them, it has become easier for me to notice the students and how little they are. How much they may have experienced in their young lives. I sometimes missed this when I was still in the classroom because I was so wrapped up in all the management of the initiatives and teaching the content and classroom management. This moment with the little girl gave me a huge reminder of how so many people are going through things that nobody else knows, and how we could use a little more empathy and humility with each other.

## THE TEACHER'S KID

### TRENT NAN, AGE 17

Honestly, I can't completely say that I know when I started feeling misunderstood. What I do know is that my OCD structured my self-discipline when I first entered the school setting, and that was a misunderstanding in itself. It was the view that others had of me from the very start. I was the "teacher's kid." I came from a "good" family. I am a "Nan." It was listening to the compliments for my good behavior that would slowly settle into my mind. The way that I was pointed out as the model for good choices. It was the pride that was taken in me as I lined up correctly without talking. It was everything. I didn't realize that I was anxious at the time. I was little, and I went to school trying to do everything right, perfect. I felt pretty good about myself in kindergarten. I learned easily, and my teacher was proud of my work, of me. I would get frustrated at times because I couldn't get things just right, but my teacher would help me through it all. In first grade, I was able to make my teacher happy most of the time. I worked hard at getting all the answers correct, and I tried to do everything I was told to do. She would always tell my mom how good I was and even called her to stop by the classroom to see my work. The pressure was starting, and I didn't know what to do.

One time my teacher was so impressed by the tower that I created that she called my mom to come and see. She told my mom that I was the only one that thought to make crossbars to create a solid foundation for my structure. She went on to say that I may grow up to be an engineer one day. As the day went on, I kept thinking about my tower. There was so much wrong with it, and no one else saw the flaws. They were so happy. They were so proud. I remember analyzing it and thinking of all the things that needed to be better. By the time I got home, I had become so frustrated with myself, with my thoughts. When my mom asked me to tell my dad about the tower, all I could say was that I was never going to be an engineer. I was so upset, and they couldn't understand why this was my reaction. All they could see was the good, and all I could see were the flaws. The imperfections were countless, and I couldn't think of one good thing to say. Just having them be happy for me somehow triggered my anxiety as if they didn't know all my faults in order to be disappointed.

By the time I was in second grade, I was starting to make mistakes. Sometimes I would talk when I shouldn't, or I would get an answer wrong. Not very often, but this really bothered me. I would keep thinking about it all day until I could get to my mom's classroom to talk with her. She would make it better, but then I would find myself feeling the same way again. She would make it better again, but it didn't last. It isn't like it is now where I can see it for what it is, but at the same time, I don't think I was as anxious as I am now. Or maybe it is just that I know what anxiety feels like, and so now I am more aware.

Whatever my teachers told me to do, I did. Partly because I was raised well, so I knew how to behave, and partly because there was always fear and worry of "what if."

*What if I ask a question, and others feel it is dumb?*

*What if I ask to go to the nurse for an upset stomach, and she thinks that I am lying?*

*Or am I really lying, and I just missed class on purpose?*

This is the game that OCD played with my world, even at a very young age. The thing is, at a young age, I didn't realize or understand my anxiety, so I kept it to myself. I was too afraid to share it, but what happened was that it just kept getting worse, and my fears became bigger and bigger, even bigger than me!

I found a method to help soothe my mind, one of repetitions. Sometimes that meant asking my mom things over and over. Other times it meant checking things to make sure that I did it. At first, this soothed my mind, but then I found myself needing it more and more. I needed it so much that I couldn't stop one thing to start another until I finished it. This was when my anxiety manifested into rituals, and when rituals started determining my day, my hour, my minute, my life. No one really knew, except for my mom.

Then came third grade. Over a couple of weeks, conversations at lunch started to build. These conversations would end up being the reason why my OCD tendencies turned into full clinical status. These conversations were with an entire lunch group. We were all witnesses to repeated conversations that we were simply not old enough to grasp. The difference between my friends and me was that they went home and left it at the lunch table and I carried it with me all day and night. Every conversation added to the one before, and I grew more anxious as the weeks went by. If only I could be like my friends.

*Why weren't they as worried as me?*

*What was wrong with me?*

My worries seemed so little compared to others. People would say, "Just don't worry." Not only didn't this work, but it made my worry worse because it was a reminder that I couldn't stop something that seemed so easy for others.

When it comes to thinking about my junior high years, I sum it up as hell with a side of learning. The environment was not the best for me to grow up in and learn at the same time. Kids at that age are like putty, being molded. And I was being molded into something that I didn't like. Some of it was my OCD, some of it was my behavior by choice, but the biggest part was what others wanted of me that started controlling my every thought and action. Things were out of my control just when I thought I could control them the most. My OCD was thriving, and at times, it was like I was OCD's complacent sidekick.

Certain things triggered my anxiety, and I felt like others knew my triggers. The truth is:

*I know you know my mom.*

*I know you know my nana.*

*I am still going to do what I am going to do.*

*Why? Because I became obsessed with rebelling.*

Some may think that it was a choice. It confuses me too. At times, I know that it was an obsession that took over, and other times my OCD wants me to think it was me. Now, I know better.

Being a teacher's kid was a huge challenge for me. When I was younger, it was hard because my mom always had an insight into what things should look like. This frustrated me terribly. Even if she knew how my math should look, or if she had a better method, I couldn't embrace her way because it wasn't the way that I was being taught in class. This would make me question my mother's knowledge and also that of my teachers, and the questioning would repeat over and over again.

After establishing I guess what some might say is a bad rep, I started to really pop up on the teachers' radar. I'm not saying that they didn't have a reason for this, but I felt singled out and not for a good reason. Then if I did something wrong, they would seemingly always bring up, "Wait till your mom or nana hear about this." Not only did this embarrass me in front of my friends—but it also embarrassed my family, especially my mom and nana, as they were such a big part of the school district I was learning in.

Although this seems like it would make me stop making these bad choices to prevent unnecessary stress on my family, I didn't. Not because I didn't care about them, but because I became obsessed with equality, or at least my definition of it. The equal grounds for respect. I started to enjoy rebelling against any authoritative figure in the school who I didn't think treated me with the same mutual respect that I was supposed to be showing them.

This is an important note because this idea of being treated with respect in return for respect really stuck with my OCD. I don't remember when I started to notice this obsession in my OCD, but I do know that it lasted for most of my sixth-grade year through the beginning of eighth grade. Keep in mind that my parents raised me to respect my elders. This became a major issue for me because there were times that I was treated with disrespect, but when I would try and tell my parents, they would side with that of the teachers and authority. They felt that even though I may have a point that I didn't have the right to share it. That I needed to be compliant even when I wasn't being treated fairly. This was like pouring gasoline on a fire because now my resentment was carrying into my home. It was impacting my relationship with everyone. I resented my parents for taking the teachers' sides, and I resented the teachers for not seeing mine. At times it made me feel awful, and other times, my OCD kept telling me I was winning. I'm not proud of the disrespect I showed anyone, ever. I am not proud of how I disrespected my teachers, nor am I saying that my logic was completely right. But at the time, my OCD found the idea that I assume would have been forgotten by most people and used it as my reasoning or motive for my deliberate insubordination.

What do I mean when I say the thought stuck with my OCD? I mean that my OCD would find something that I may have been insecure about or felt strong enough about, and it became a non-stop obsession that led to compulsions that aren't there for most people. I guess that's why it's called a disorder.

I was a typical middle schooler in many ways. Just like others, I couldn't control my home life. What others thought was a perfect family was extremely challenging for me. My parents had reasonable expectations, but the ones that did not match mine and OCD thrived on this conflict. I was a rebellious teen with OCD on my side. I picked every battle I could. Most I lost, but that only encouraged me to fight more. My parents were always on the side of the school and every adult. Don't get me wrong;

they were always in my corner, helping me to be better, but that wasn't enough for me. They would listen to me speak, but in the end, I was reminded of my upbringing and to respect the adults in charge. "Respect your elders" only damaged my view of them and fixated my attention on the unfairness of being a kid.

The social aspect can be decided for the most part at that age. I turned to my friends for everything, good and bad. No matter how awkward you are or anti-social you are in middle school, you can find friends; it just takes conformity at times. For me, friends were easiest during those years and kept me from completely dreading school. This was an area that my OCD enjoyed, because who I talked to within my school day was out of control of my parents and teachers alike. Each time I had to hear that my mom was one phone call away was just a trigger to give them a reason to call.

What was out of my control and affected me the most were the teachers that I had in class. Your teachers shouldn't be something that you feel are out of your control, like *how did I get stuck in this situation?* To me, a kid's school life should be the last thing to stress them out, and yet it does if you feel stuck.

Some of the teachers were really there for me. Whether they understood or not in the beginning, they tried to understand by the end. They were willing to work through situations with me. Mrs. Steff, my eighth grade Language Arts teacher, was ready to fight for me before I even knew it. She would reach out to my mom and ask more about my OCD. My mom would give her advice, and she would take it and use it to help me. One time I got really stuck on the unfairness of an assignment. She wanted me to "Bingo" read a variety of books for the nine weeks. This meant

I had to pick and choose different genres, even if I didn't like them. I couldn't understand the point of this assignment. I was able to read anything at my reading level and beyond, yet I was being forced to waste my time reading things I had no interest in, and this became an issue for me, but mostly for my OCD. After weeks of irritation, my mom stepped in and asked me what it was that I wanted. What solution could I offer and still meet the required amount of reading? I told her if I had to read, I at least wanted to read something I liked and had an interest in. It wasn't really about Mrs. Steff; it was a build-up of resentment towards the system for making me read and take assessments just to do it. This had been going on for years. It never mattered that I was reading years beyond my grade level; I still had to read what everyone else was reading. It didn't matter that I processed things quickly—I had to keep pace with my peers, and it led to boredom and resentment. This was just another assignment that wasn't about me but about the system. My mom encouraged me to talk to my teacher, and so I did. Mrs. Steff was amazing. She told me that if I wanted to read a fishing magazine, she would allow it, as long as I was reading. This was everything to me and to the relationship I was building with her. That one adjustment or compromise made a difference in my entire school year.

Then there were others. Those that viewed me as the student with no opinion. Ones that viewed my behavior as all choice. Ones that viewed the conflict as a personal problem that I had to figure out, and until I did, I would get punished. Ones that saw an attitude and not a disorder. That was so hard for me. I was only 10-, 11-, 12-, and 13-years-old. If I knew what was wrong or how to fix it, I would have tried. I was doing what I could do. I had a therapist to help me work on "tools for my toolbox." The problem was that I was also trying to learn to recognize when I needed those tools. If my anxiety went past a 5 on a 0 - 10 scale, I was no longer able to think clearly. At that time in my life, I could jump from a 0 to a 5 quickly and miss the signs. Once that happened, I needed adults to help me. I felt that my teachers could have worked with me one-on-one and helped me to figure out what was going on, but it felt to me it was easier to get me out of their space. Another problem was that I didn't feel I had a safe place to go when I was anxious in the earlier years of my junior high experience. I needed to be able to vent and let out my emotions in order to gain control, but in school, that could come with a consequence. At that point, I felt like I didn't have anywhere to turn, so I just let it out wherever I was.

Once I had a teacher tell me, I knew a lot about nothing. What does that even mean? I was completely into the lesson that was being taught and couldn't wait to share what I knew. I know it wasn't part of the material we were covering, but this unit had my attention because it revolved around my interest in science. How did I go from being gifted to not knowing anything?

This stuck. Hard.

*Doesn't my teacher want to know what I know?*
*Does this mean I'm not gifted anymore?*
*What is my IQ?*

I was determined to find out. I needed to know if I really knew something or not. This became my next obsession until another teacher told me I was heading down "the gifted hole."

*What does that mean?*

*Will I ever be able to get out?*

These thoughts were overwhelming. They stayed in my head day and night. Learning started to come second, and sometimes third. This led to teachers telling me I was smarter than I was showing in class. I should be achieving higher than how I performed. I was starting to question everything. My thoughts were consumed with worry, and I was unable to be the person everyone expected me to be. The only thing that came easy was my OCD.

OCD is hard enough on a "normal" day. It's even harder on a rough day, as one might imagine. But for me, I would have small things at the beginning of my days that would stick with me and fuel a fire that the teachers weren't exactly eager to extinguish, but rather pour gasoline all over it.

I had some teachers at the beginning that didn't choose to understand my situation but came around, in the end, to appreciate that it was the best for both of us—not only for my learning experience but for their teaching experience too. I had some who saw the good in me and gave me the safe place that I needed. Those teachers are the ones who made a big difference in my life. They are the ones I choose to remember.

## MY LITTLE FOOT

SOPHIA M. BAKER, AGE 11

I have had a big struggle all my life. It started when I was still in my mother's stomach, waiting to be born. Before I was born, my parent's car crashed, and my egg sack ripped, and a part of it wrapped around my left foot and prevented it from growing. It also wrapped around my right ankle, leaving a zig-zag-like mark around it.

Now my little foot was only the bottom half of a normal foot. But, to me, since everything is different, I guess everything is also in one way normal to me. This little foot may be little, but it is very strong. There are many up-sides about having amniotic band syndrome (or a little foot is an easier way to say it).

Some of those up-sides are things like not feeling anything when you kick things like breaking a wooden board and having great balance. But there are a lot of struggles too. First of all, the reason I can't stub my toes when I kick things is that I don't have toes on that foot. I couldn't keep my toes because they were a big problem! I got blisters and bruises and scars. Every time my toes would get stuck in blanket threads, and when I woke up, all of my sleep struggling had tied the thread to my toes, so a few months later, the doctors had to use a machine to cut them off. Also, another struggle I have is that all my life, from preschool to fifth grade, I've been made fun of, and not just my little foot but other things too. Like, for example, glasses, shoes, hair, clothes and other things! But the worst struggle is still my little foot.

Sure, I'm proud of being different, but I'm not proud of being made fun of. Ever since first grade, kids have been calling my foot names like slimy, sticky, scary, small, infected, slow, weird, creepy, and many more. But, at least now, I have prosthetics that help me with running, turning, jumping, kicking, and balance.

I am about to end my story now, but before I do, I want everyone to know that they should be proud of their differences, and you can achieve great things!

## LIFE BEYOND FEAR

### BY MARIE, AGE 11

My family situation all started when I was about five-years-old, and I started realizing that my father was not the same playful person that I remembered. He started to sleep more, and he didn't do as much with me as he used to, and it was getting worse. I didn't tell anyone other than my friend who was going through something, too.

At this time, I wish I'd told my teachers and talked to them, but when it was happening, I thought it was normal. But, one day I went over to my best friend's house. I was going to spend the night, but it was my first sleepover in a long time, and I was scared, so I called my mom. She came and picked me up. When we got home, the door was locked. We kept ringing the doorbell, and no one came. So, we sat outside for just a few moments, and I was at the time thinking *wait, why would my dad not let us in the house*. Me, my sister, and my mom were outside, but my brother was inside. I remember my mom saying, "I'm going to be right back." She went around the house, broke the glass on the door, and then next thing I knew, my brother unlocked the front door, and my dad was following him. My brother told us to go inside, so we did, but then my dad was there, so we ran back outside. I didn't know what was happening, so I sat down, waiting for my mom. When she came back, we drove off.

We were trying to find somewhere to stay for the night, and

one of our friends said we could stay at their place, so we stayed the night there. It was odd, and I found out what was happening; my dad had started to drink. I was confused at first but slowly started to figure out what was happening.

Years went on, and it got worse. My teachers found out, but I still thought it wasn't that big of a deal. I kept telling myself that everything was good. My teacher talked to me about it. They asked if I was fine, and I always said yes, even though, really, I wasn't. In 2016, it got really bad. Our friend said they had a guest house we could stay in. So, for two or three days, we cleaned the house. The police officer who lived next to us got our dad out of the house so we could grab our things. When we got to the house we were going to stay in, we unpacked and spent some time there.

I remember trying to go to bed that night thinking about if what we were doing was right or not. Weeks went on. I saw my dad multiple times when we would drive past. Then one day, our friend said she would take my sister and me to see him at Taco Bell. So, we decided we would go. It was very odd, but after we ate at Taco Bell, he brought us to the house he was staying at. I was really excited when I got to see all of my pets that we had to leave when we switched houses. We picked up some of our things. Our room looked the same from when we left, but it felt different. Our dad gave us stuff we really did not need, but for some reason, we took it. We were meeting the person who took us to the church my dad preached at. She picked us up, dropped us off, and helped get our things out of the car that our dad gave us. When we got back to where we were staying, my mom talked to us and asked how it was. I told her it was fine, and she just kept asking questions, and I kept answering, but in my mind, I was like, "Just let me be, please." I understood why she was asking, but it was hard, and it is still hard today.

A year went by. We moved back in with my father, but it was still getting worse, so we got a protective order. My teachers tried to be there, but I pushed them away except for one, my old social studies teacher. She was always there for me, even though I tried to not say what I was feeling. Then once I did start talking to my teacher, it got so much easier. I still didn't talk to her a lot unless something was bugging me.

Then, I realized we were going to move. I knew my mom wanted to move, but I didn't. I was at that school since pre-k, so moving was something I did not want to do. So, once again, I did not tell anyone other than my two best friends and my social studies teacher. I spent so much time hiding out in my room watching YouTube videos. I was so tired, and I felt like I couldn't keep my head above water. I started only wanting to sit in my room more and more and not do my schoolwork at home, so I did it in every class I got a chance to, so I didn't have to take it home.

One of my teachers started to think something was wrong. Then my teachers decided to try to talk to me about what was going on. I told them that we were going to most likely move and that this was going to be the last year at that school. They told me to start telling them when something was bugging me. I said I would, but to be honest, I never did tell them if something was bothering me—unless I knew they were going to find out, then I did tell them. School stayed the same, but at home, it got different. My mom was looking for a new place to live; my sister and brother stopped playing with me as much. I felt like I was alone. I started wishing I told my teachers, but it was too late. Well, that is what I told myself, at least. I didn't tell my mom, my sister, or my brother, so I tried my best to act okay. My teachers stopped asking as many questions about how I was feeling, so the year felt kind of normal. It was around April when my mom decided to get a divorce. It was hard, but I was happy to get it over with. So, they got a divorce.

When that happened, my mom really wanted to find a new house, and she applied for many jobs. Then when she got an offer, she accepted it. We looked at houses and found one we liked. We finished school that year and then moved at the end of summer.

From everything I have been through, I have learned that there is always someone there for you, and you should not push them away. Don’t be afraid to tell someone what you are going through. Don't hide from what scares you or what makes you worried, but let it strengthen you and let it make you stronger. Thank you to everyone who was there for me when I needed it, especially all my friends who understood I needed them even when I said I didn't.

## SPEEDBUMPS AND ROADBLOCKS

### CASSY DEBACCO, AGE 18

Mental health is an extremely important topic that should be discussed in every single school. The stigma attached to mental illness is very alarming, and I have personally felt this stigma affects my life. I had struggled to come forward and ask for help when I knew I needed it. I have instead struggled in silence, hoping for something to change instead of taking the actions needed to help myself. Learning how to manage my mental health in school is not only important but essential to being able to function on a day-to-day basis. I struggle with anxiety and depression. I have been diagnosed with general anxiety, but my actual diagnosis doesn't matter. All that matters is that I struggle with my mental health and that the thoughts I have affect how I function every day, especially at school. I spend the majority of my day inside school. I often stay after school to get help from teachers or attend club meetings. I spend more time at school than I do in my own house each day.

I realized early on that I had a very overactive brain. I could start to feel it affecting my life in seventh and eighth grade. During those years, not only did I have to deal with the challenges of fitting in, popularity, and learning all about life and the other *finding yourself* issues that you deal with at those younger ages, I also had to learn how to deal with high-functioning anxiety. After realizing that my anxious thoughts weren't healthy, I did reach out to my guidance counselor in the eighth grade. I'm so happy that I did because it has put me on the path that I am on today. She connected me with the school therapist. At first, I was very uneasy about this. I had no idea what to expect, and I wasn't confident that talking to someone was even going to help. However, I knew something needed to change, so I started to meet with that school counselor weekly during school. That was the first exposure I ever had to therapy. Although I realized that that specific therapist was not the best option for me, I recognized how valuable therapy is. I wanted to continue therapy outside of the school, so my next step was to ever so boldly ask my mother if I could go see a different therapist. Up until that point, I had never told her about all of the struggles I had been having. Sometimes opening up to the people closest to me (my family) is the hardest part. I didn't want to be seen as weak or a failure. Before seeing the school counselor, I had no idea that the school even offered those services and that I could get counseling right there at the school if I wanted to. I wish that students were made aware of this option and that it wasn't so secretive. It's okay to get help, but it's that stigma that makes it feel like you should be ashamed in school when you need to go to guidance. It is nothing to be embarrassed about or feel guilty about; it's a sign of strength when you seek help for yourself.

I began going to therapy outside of school every week or two weeks, and it helped a lot! I learned a lot about myself and how it's okay to not be okay. My first time going to therapy was honestly terrifying. It was a really hard time for me. Not only was I already struggling with these overwhelming thoughts in my head, but now I had to figure out the words and say it all out loud to someone that I didn't even know. But as I began going to therapy, I realized the value of working out my thoughts with a professional. I learned different breathing techniques; I learned how to sort out rational and irrational thoughts as well as healthy and unhealthy thoughts. I was introduced to so many different videos, books, apps, and more that have also helped me. Simply talking to someone who just "got" what I was going through and didn't judge me for it was so beneficial. I could talk to someone who understood what I was feeling and could help me with my struggles.

But it was still really hard for me to go to school. I love school and always have. Unfortunately, I know that is not a common opinion among other students. However, I love learning, and I love the challenge of my academic classes. I am a math geek through and through. So whenever my anxiety started to affect how I felt and how I functioned in school, it was really hard to navigate that and to accept it. I was constantly mind-reading, thinking that everyone hated me or was making fun of me. Every time I gave an answer in class, I immediately felt silly and embarrassed. I started to not speak in class, even when I had so much to say. I always second-guessed myself and was too scared. I also had to deal with panic attacks and trying not to have one during school. I really didn't know how to handle all of those feelings during school. I felt there was no system in place that allowed me to escape if I needed to. Many students would abuse such an escape route. If given a chance to escape the classroom, some students would do it more often than necessary, taking advantage of something so greatly needed. Students, such as myself, would then start to feel self-conscious about leaving because they would then fear that people would think they were abusing the system as well.

As I continued going through high school, 9th, 10th, 11th, and now 12th grade, I had switched therapists, went on and off medication, and had switched psychiatrists. As I began to dive deeper into my therapy, what I needed out of going to therapy changed. I had changed as a person, and I was beginning to feel stuck. I wasn't making progress anymore. I felt it would be best to find someone else who I could benefit from the most. At first, I was so nervous about my decision to switch, but I am so glad I did. I was lucky that I found a therapist I liked on my second try. It takes some people a lot longer until they find someone that they feel comfortable with. I feel that is one of the most important parts of therapy. If you aren't comfortable, you won't get what you need out of the experience. I also found people and friends who I felt comfortable reaching out to as well, but I was still trying to figure out how to deal with my anxiety during school. I used different breathing techniques that I had learned to help me through the day. I also learned to sort through my thoughts and learn when they were unhealthy and irrational. I often have no evidence for all the anxious and self-deprecating thoughts I have. I try to focus on the evidence and not make up situations in my head. However, I am a senior this year, and I am still trying to figure out the best way to handle my mental health during school hours. But I would really like to talk about this year because during this year, even over the past couple of weeks, a lot of things changed for me. I learned a lot about what I can do for myself during school.

This year has been really difficult for me. The stress of

applying and selecting a college has weighed on me heavily. The fear of the unknown and immensity of the future has increased my anxiety to high levels. My depression has been a roller coaster where some days I am feeling great, and other days, I feel like I've hit rock bottom, only to discover that there is a lower bottom to hit. It has been extremely frustrating to still feel so anxious and low in my senior year of high school. I've been dealing with this for so long I thought I would have fewer lows, and they wouldn't be as bad. I thought I would be having more highs and experiencing more joy, not less. Or maybe I thought that's how I was supposed to be feeling.

My therapist and my medication have been helping me through my anxious and depressive thoughts, but school has still been a challenge. I am so fearful as to how other people look at me. I'm afraid they can tell how anxious I am. I've participated less in class. I almost feel like I'm not even present for most of the day during school. I've described walking into school as having the wind knocked out of me because my anxiety is that bad. I just get this overwhelming feeling of negativity and fear. I don't even need to have wild thoughts in my head, and I still feel the physical symptoms of anxiety. I am constantly surrounded by my peers, which makes me feel like I have to put on a fake smile and be a certain person who I am not. When I have really bad days or I feel a panic attack coming on, I feel trapped and alone. I don't know what to do in those situations without drawing unwanted attention to myself. I often feel ashamed, embarrassed, and guilty for feeling the way that I do. Because even though I believe the stigma attached to mental health is horrible and needs to be fixed, I can feel the effects when I am at school. I am surrounded by students who are uneducated about mental illnesses because it is not talked about at school as much as it should be.

~

As I woke up one day getting ready for school, I knew I was feeling off. Some days I can feel really great and confident, ready, and excited for the day ahead, but this day I felt so hopeless and defeated. I still drove myself to school and went to first period. But as I sat there, listening and trying to learn, I knew I couldn't do it anymore. I asked to go to the nurse, but instead, I went to a trusted teacher's classroom. I cried to her and told her the scary and horrible thoughts I had been having. Then my guidance counselor, who I also trust very much, got involved, and we figured out the steps I should take from there. Even though that was an extremely hard day for me, I am glad I had such wonderful people in the school who I felt safe enough to talk to. After that day, I have continued to talk with that trusted teacher, keeping her informed and updated about me. Together, we wrote an email to all of my teachers. I wanted my teachers to know a little bit about what I had been going through recently. I wanted them to know that if I missed class or seemed disengaged during class, there was a reason why. I included that if they would like to talk to me more about this, then I would be willing to discuss it with them.

This email has given me so much reassurance, and I wish I would have done it earlier in high school. I received responses back from my teachers, telling me to let them know whatever I need. And it made me feel less guilty for feeling the way I do during class. I think this is a great thing for all students to do when they are going through a difficult time or are struggling with something so personal. It is important to put your mental health above everything else, a hard but important lesson I've had to learn. You can't be your best self for others if you don't take care of yourself first. I wish I had done this years ago. The teachers at my school have all been so understanding. Having strong teacher-to-student relationships in school is imperative. Of course, it is important to learn in school, but while we, the students are in school, we are also figuring out who we are. Schools should be supportive and safe, a place where students can receive emotional support from adults they trust. I feel like it helps to know that someone in the room with you knows what's been going on.

I hope that every student could be as lucky as I am to have such incredible educators who genuinely care about my well-being. And for students who can't think of someone they can reach out to, I would say to take the risk and start talking with the teacher of your favorite class or the teacher you have the most in common with. Start with having normal conversations until you can build that relationship up enough where you can open up more to them. It has made all the difference for me. It is so important for educators to be more than just a teacher, but for them to be a support system for their students and a safe space.

However, I still continued to struggle. As part of our senior course of study, we have to prepare a portfolio of our work and complete a senior "mock" interview. It is a great way to introduce students to how interviews will be for them in the future. On the day of my interview, probably because of the stress of the interview and other overwhelming tasks looming over me, I had a panic attack during school. I hadn't had one for a while, and I can't even remember when the last time I had one during school was. I hid out in that same trusted teacher's room, missing my first and second period, waiting for it to pass. Recently, I also had a panic attack during my calculus class, my favorite class of the day. It's even hard to pinpoint why I felt so anxious and nervous during the class, but I did. I couldn't breathe, and I had my face in my hands for the whole class period. When the class was over and the other students left, I stayed, and my teacher sat in the room with me until I could breathe again. I am so grateful he was so understanding.

I am graduating at the top of my class with an amazing scholarship to Elizabethtown College next year. I just wish there was more of a system in place for kids like me who go through some of the same things as I do. I wish there was a way to be able to exit a class when the anxiety is just too bad. I wish there was a way to tell my teachers that I'm having a bad day, so they don't call on me during class without having to share every single detail of my life with them. For those students who aren't as lucky as I am, and don't have that trusted teacher or an adult they feel they can go to, I hope that they are made aware of the resources available to them. I hope mental health becomes more of a focus for schools and that plenty of programs, support groups, therapists, and other resources become known for all students. Part of the solution is to be aware of what is happening. Don't ignore these issues and realize that you never know how a student may need help, so be there for them.

My mental illness does not make me weak, it makes me

strong. It does not make me weird or a freak, it makes me human. It does not make me any less capable. I hope that the stigma attached to mental illness goes away because that is one of the biggest obstacles for students who need help. I believe schools have a huge role to play in this change. As I said before, I spend more of my day in school than out of it. I also feel teachers also have a responsibility to create a supportive environment for the students to feel comfortable asking for help. This will be life-changing in more ways than one. I can't wait to see the amazing changes that I know schools will be making in the future and how students' lives will change. I can't wait to see how society will change, and the stigma attached to mental illnesses will disappear. I can't wait to say, "Look how far we've come." Most importantly, I look forward to seeing where I go in the future. I am so excited to be able to look back and say, "Look how far **I've** come."

# CONCLUSION

If you've read my book *The Fire Within,* you may remember that the first quote in the book is from *Harry Potter*. Dumbledore says, "Happiness can be found, even in the darkest of times, if one only remembers to turn on the light." What I love about this quote is that it isn't magic that turns on the light. It's not a student or another magical creature. It's not one of the people from the Ministry of Magic or some unicorn from the forest. One must remember to *turn on the light themselves*. When we discuss educator engagement, this same principle applies. If we are waiting around for someone else to re-engage us, it's simply not going to happen. We are responsible for our own lights, if only we remember to find it and turn it on.

Educator engagement is a topic that is close to my heart. Being a part of the education community has been a gift in my life, and my heart breaks when I work with districts and see the hollowed-out faces of educators when I know that there used to be light and a spark. I know that it is possible to re-engage, and writing this book to help educators find their way is one of the most important parts of my purpose. As educators, we deserve to be happy. We will get there when we learn to expect it.

There are multiple reasons that disengagement can happen. Any combination of personal or professional adversities, burnout, secondary traumatic stress, teacher trauma, or demoralization can be the catalyst and weight that can drag a person down the disengaged side of the educator engagement continuum. However, having the words to give our emotions and understanding these concepts is one of the first steps in recognizing when they're happening and fighting against it.

Our brains and bodies play a part in both negativity and positivity and how we perpetuate each. Our brains have no moral compass. They will make the connections for whatever we do the most. Speak negatively and unkindly, then that's what your brain will support you in doing more of. Speak kindly and feel gratitude, and your brain will rewire itself for that. It's not easy to make that change, but practicing gratitude and creating positive intentions is a great way to get started. You decide. You tell your brain what connections to make. It's one of the things we actually have control over.

When we are fighting stress and having negative thoughts, mindfulness and self-care can help us heal. They're not going to be our only saviors. Sometimes, professional help is necessary. But practicing mindfulness with intention and implementing self-care routines that address the physical, mental, emotional, and spiritual sides will allow for a more holistic approach to maintaining that balance.

Finally, there are activities that we can do to re-engage or stay engaged. Finding purpose and core beliefs will tether you to education and help hold you up during adversity. Reflecting, creating relationships, and finding a passion area will create an emotional connection that you may have lost. Create goals, ones you really want to actually meet, and then meet them! It will feel amazing, and those quick wins will bring you such joy.

The most important part is to remember that you're not alone in this. I promise you, whether you are feeling disengaged, negative emotional engagement, or even if you are feeling fully engaged, you are not alone. You are not the only one feeling apathetic, or feeling like you want to fight but you don't know how, and you're not sure if you'll make a difference. If you're fully engaged, you are not the only one who is still feeling positive and excited about teaching, even when it seems like those around you may not be feeling the same way. There are others out there like you. Find them. Find your people. We are in this profession because we love to connect and reach others. There may be times when it feels appropriate to cut people out. It's not. When you feel like you need to put yourself in a silo, that's when you need those people the most.

Being an educator is difficult, but we are not meant to be martyrs. We are not meant to be unhappy or angry or disconnected. Hypothetically, we have the potential to work in the happiest profession in the world. We have the opportunity to shape a child's life. We can be the turning point in a students' life who is struggling with an alcoholic father or mental health issues of their own. Amazingly, we have that kind of power in another human's existence. By ensuring our own engagement and by helping those around us, we are working toward our own happiness and the calling that we felt that day we stepped into our very first classroom.

# REFERENCES

Administration of Children and Families. (n.d.). Secondary traumatic stress. Retrieved November 30, 2019, from https://www.acf.hhs.gov/trauma-toolkit/secondary-traumatic-stress.

Brooks, H., Rushton, K., Walker, S., Lovell, K., & Rogers, A. (2016). Ontological security and connectivity provided by pets: A study in the self-management of the everyday lives of people diagnosed with a long-term mental health condition. *BMC Psychiatry, 16*(1). doi: 10.1186/s12888-016-1111-3

Defining mindfulness. (2017, January 11). Retrieved January 22, 2020, from https://www.mindful.org/jon-kabat-zinn-defining-mindfulness/

Desroches, S.M. (2013), Exploring teacher turnover in American-accredited schools in South America. Theses and Dissertations. Paper 1473

Ellison, L. L. (2017). Emotional disengagement. *The SAGE Encyclopedia of Marriage, Family, and Couples Counseling, 2,* 513–517. doi: 10.4135/9781483369532.n160

Figley, Cr. (1999). Secondary traumatic stress: Self-care issues for clinicians, researchers, and educators. Compassion fatigue: Toward a new understanding of the cost of caring. 3-28.

Froehlich, M. B. (2018). *Divergent EDU.* EduMatch Publishing.

Gotter, A. (2019, February 27). Low testosterone in men. Retrieved January 22, 2020, from https://www.healthline.com/health/side-effects-of-low-testosterone

Hanna, R., & Pennington, K. (2015, January 8). Despite reports to the contrary, new teachers are staying in their jobs longer. Retrieved November 25, 2019, from https://www.americanprogress.org/issues/education-k-12/news/2015/01/08/103421/despite-reports-to-the-contrary-new-teachers-are-staying-in-their-jobs-longer/.

Karsenti1, T., & Collin, S. (2013). Why are new teachers leaving the profession? Results of a Canada-wide survey. *Education, 3*(3), 141–149. doi: 10.5923/j.edu.20130303.01

Korb, A. (2012, November 20). The grateful brain. Retrieved January 24, 2020, from https://www.psychologytoday.com/us/blog/prefrontal-nudity/201211/the-grateful-brain

Kruse, K. (2012, June 22). What is employee engagement? *Forbes*. Retrieved from https://www.forbes.com/sites/kevinkruse/2012/06/22/employee-engagement-what-and-why/#788c63827f37

Magids, S., Zorfas, A., & Leemon, D. (2019, September 23). The new science of customer emotions. *Harvard Business Review*. Retrieved November 24, 2019, from https://hbr.org/2015/11/the-new-science-of-customer-emotions.

National Child Traumatic Stress Network, Secondary Traumatic Stress Committee. (2011). Secondary traumatic stress: A fact sheet for child-serving professionals. Los Angeles, CA, and Durham, NC: National Center for Child Traumatic Stress.

Onderko, K. (2018, November 13). What is trauma? - Definition, symptoms, responses, types & therapy. Retrieved November 26, 2019, from https://integratedlistening.com/what-is-trauma/.

Peterson, S. (2018). Secondary traumatic stress. Retrieved November 30, 2019, from https://www.nctsn.org/trauma-informed-care/secondary-traumatic-stress.

Pietrangelo, S., & Watson, S. (2018, September 29). The effects of stress on your body. Retrieved January 22, 2020, from https://www.healthline.com/health/stress/effects-on-body#1

Porges, S.W. The polyvagal theory: New insights into adaptive reactions of the autonomic nervous system. Cleveland Clinic Journal of Medicine, 76(Suppl 2), S86–S90, 2009.

Ruiz, R. (2014). How childhood trauma could be mistaken for ADHD. Retrieved January 22, 2020, from https://www.theatlantic.com/health/archive/2014/07/how-childhood-trauma-could-be-mistaken-for-adhd/373328/

Santoro, D. A. (2018). *Demoralized: why teachers leave the profession they love and how they can stay*. Cambridge, MA: Harvard Education Press.

Scaccia, A. (2017, May 18). Serotonin: What you need to know. Retrieved January 23, 2020, from Healthline: https://www.healthline.com/health/mental-health/serotonin#overview1

Singh, D. (2018). *Purposeful hustle: Direct your life's work toward making a positive impact*. BookBaby.

Singhal, P. (2017, June 6). Why up to half of all Australian teachers are quitting within five years. Retrieved November 25, 2019, from https://www.smh.com.au/education/why-up-to-half-of-all-australian-teachers-are-quitting-within-five-years-20170605-gwks31.html.

Solan, M. (2016, April 27). Back to school: Learning a new skill can slow cognitive aging. Retrieved January 22, 2020, from https://www.health.harvard.edu/blog/learning-new-skill-can-slow-cognitive-aging-201604279502

Van Der Kolk, B. A. (2015). *The body keeps the score: Mind, brain, and body in the transformation of trauma.* London: Penguin Books.

Watson, M., & Kissane, D. W. (2017). *Management of clinical depression and anxiety*. New York, NY: Oxford University Press. doi: 10.1093/med/9780190491857.001.0001

Weale, S. (2016, October 24). Almost a third of teachers quit state sector within five years of qualifying. Retrieved November 25, 2019, from https://www.theguardian.com/education/2016/oct/24/almost-third-of-teachers-quit-within-five-years-of-qualifying-figures.

Whitaker, L. (2018, May 3). How does thinking positive thoughts affect neuroplasticity? Retrieved January 24, 2020, from https://meteoreducation.com/how-does-thinking-positive-thoughts-affect-neuroplasticity/

World Health Organization (n.d.) *International Classification of Diseases*. Retrieved November 30, 2019, from https://icd.who.int/browse11/l-m/en#/http://id.who.int/icd/entity/129180281.

# BIOGRAPHY

Mandy Froehlich passionately encourages educators to create innovative change in their classrooms. A former Director of Innovation and Technology, technology integrator, and teacher, she has experience at many levels of the organizational structure. Currently, as a full-time consultant, keynote speaker, and presenter, her interest lies in reinvigorating and re-engaging teachers back into their profession, as well as what's needed to support teachers in their pursuit of innovative and divergent thinking and teaching. She consults internationally with school districts and post-secondary institutions in the effective use of technology to support great teaching, mental health support for educators, and how to create organizational change. Her first book, *The Fire Within: Lessons from defeat that have ignited a passion for learning,* discusses mental health awareness for teachers. Her second book, Divergent EDU, is based on an organizational structure she developed to support teachers in innovative and divergent thinking. All of her books can be found on Amazon and Barnes and Noble in both digital and print formats.

ALSO BY MANDY FROEHLICH

THE FIRE WITHIN

DIVERGENTEDU

EduMatch Publishing

CPSIA information can be obtained
at www.ICGtesting.com
Printed in the USA
BVHW041658070520
579381BV00010B/96

9 781970 133745